A MIGHTY STORM

Stories Of Resilience After Irene

A MIGHTY STORM

Stories Of Resilience After Irene

Copyright © 2011 by Yvonne Daley and The Rutland Herald

Project Editor Rob Mitchell, the Rutland Herald / Times Argus
Written and edited by Yvonne Daley with staff writers from the
Rutland Herald and Barre-Montpelier Times Argus
Photos by Vyto Starinskas, Jeb Wallace-Brodeur & the Rutland Herald / Times Argus staff
Cover and interior design by Debbi Wraga

ISBN Number: 978-1-60571-129-4
Library of Congress Number: 2011962320

Cover photo: *Don Fielder of Stockbridge walks on a now uneven floor in his home, which was ripped apart by floodwaters during Irene. Courtesy of Jeb Wallace-Brodeur.*

Back cover photos: Top: *Rochester residents help Jon Graham salvage what he can from his home, which he was in when it collapsed on the Sunday of Irene.* **Bottom:** *River Road in Killington was buckled and broken by Irene. Both photos courtesy of Vyto Starinskas.*

Building Community, One Book at a Time

This book was printed by the Northshire Bookstore, a family-owned, independent bookstore in Manchester Ctr., Vermont, since 1976.
Printed in the United States of America

Net proceeds from sales of the book will be split evenly among the following three charities:

- The VT Irene Flood Relief Fund, providing grants to small businesses statewide affected by the flooding in partnership with the Central Vermont Community Action Council.
- The Mobile Home Project Fund, a relief fund benefiting many of Vermont's most vulnerable residents with picking up and rebuilding after floodwaters wreaked havoc in mobile home parks across the state.
- The Rutland Relief Fund, which benefits Rutland-area residents who were hurt by flooding.

SHIRES PRESS

4869 Main Street, Manchester Center, VT 05255 • www.northshire.com/printondemand

To Bruce ~
who knows resilience

A MIGHTY STORM
Stories Of Resilience After Irene

Yvonne Daley

YVONNE DALEY

From Wilmington to Waterbury, the Deerfield River to Lake Champlain, the storm transformed Vermont.
And in the following months, Vermonters themselves.

Gordon Gifford was a resident of Weston's Trailer Park. He is taking a moment to compose himself while talking to Photographer Mark Collier about the destruction of his home.

INTRODUCTION

*W*e know that we are changed; we don't know how much.

The ground beneath our feet was literally torn away, and a lot else too. We know that our waterways, many of them just that day pleasurable streams and creeks not prone to flooding, we know they are not what they once seemed. Rivers and streams, roaring and babbling brooks – the clichés have new meaning now – these will never be just a reliable setting for the pastoral life again; those days are over for many of us for a long time. Tropical Storm Irene changed all that. The rains came, unending rains that lasted less than a day, yet dumped a deluge of rainwater. Familiar rivers and rills became something else entirely, torrents with incalculable power. In less than a workday, they carved both physical and metaphysical chasms into people and places, realigned hundreds of miles of our land, destroyed hundreds of homes and businesses.

How can water deplete bank accounts, wipe out histories, destroy memories, make friends of enemies? We learned how. But we learned other things as well. Irene delivered immeasurable sorrows but in her wake Vermonters provided ample evidence of fortitude. The days and weeks after Irene inspired ingenuity by reducing life to essentials. We learned that we can trust one another, and that we can trust one another to do the right thing. Even if Irene did not impact you or your town or your county, if you are a Vermonter, you are different, lessened, made greater, reduced, increased, broken, reconstructed by the storm and its aftermath.

We just don't know how much.

We have lived in a world in which natural disasters – tsunamis, hurricanes, earthquakes, wildfires, the background noise of disasters – has been brought to us with so much frequency that calamity almost seemed a backdrop to human life, but misfortune delivered to us from a distance, from someone else's home. With Irene, it became our turn. And so we learned again about independence while conceding our dependence. We are Vermont strong but we know our weaknesses. Drive our roads and you will see we are no longer as pretty as we once were. We will be pretty again, but right now there are places where we are down to the bone. Our future is there, overshadowed certainly by the cost of rebuilding and the deeper cost, the cost of all that cannot be made whole, brought back to life, restored to what once was. Some gained faith; some lost it.

We just don't know how much.

There are some other lessons we learned. As Irene traced its wet rampage up into the mountains, down into the villages, taking with it homes and land, reducing roads to rubble, it exposed what lay just under a thin skin of soil. We live in a tough place, but we have a tougher underside. Our state is made from boulders the size of Volkswagens but also of sand as silky as any tawny beach. I took to thinking we were seeing our glacier age revealed. Everywhere you went, people close to the torrent talked of the sound, the clashing symphony of rocks smashing against one another and the swiftness with which substantive trees were wrenched from the earth. That sound — the boulders, the trees — has become the nightmare of people like Andy Coyne of Jamaica, whose house was spared while all around him was rerouted and ravished, and Susan Mordecai, whose house was not and whose possessions became litter along a once peaceful brook.

I write these words with a heavy heart because I love Vermont and the people who live here. In the months since Aug. 28, I have seen unimaginable destruction and heard stories that have made me cry. Yet, this is somehow a positive story, another in mankind's grand history of epic courage and grit, of immeasurable munificence and creativity. For a journalist who has seen too many examples of the meanness of the human, not to mention our tendencies toward indifference and exploitation, the days and weeks since Irene have brought with them another river, a river of stories that demonstrate that the human is good, that Vermonters are indeed different, that a life lived close to the land brings with it sadness and loss but that it also feeds us. It is why we are still here.

And why we know that we are changed; we just don't know how much.

YVONNE DALEY

WAVES IN THE WOOD

By Verandah Porche and Patty Carpenter

River, it was risin', footing lost in the storm.
Strange, what matters when flood sweeps over the corn.
Fields disappearing; house might follow suit.
What's left to harvest? Stones where there once was fruit.

Head for the hills, darling, river's at our door.
Waves in the wood. You hear them roar?
That was the stream we waded yesterday.
Kissed on the rocks. Takes my breath away…

Friends 'n' strangers gather tryin' to fix the harm.
It's a funny thing to say, "This is the best place to lose your farm."
Did you catch on YouTube: covered bridge went down?
Horse-and-rider brave the water to get medicine to town.

They call it a hundred, a hundred-year storm.
Did we turn the key; set the ocean to warm,
tornado on spin, the heartland on dry?
Tricky to prove but it's hard to deny.

Future is a gamble. Change is in the air.
Dance among the shambles, dream beyond despair.
In mother tongues I can't pronounce, our children's song resounds.
Plant a tree or stanza deep in common ground.

THE GOVERNOR'S MESSAGE TO VERMONTERS

In the days and weeks after Tropical Storm Irene roared through our state, the tally of destruction was stunning: Six lives lost, more than 500 miles of paved roads destroyed, bridges damaged or washed away entirely, well over 1,000 homes destroyed or severely damaged, businesses knocked out and rich farmland buried under contaminated silt and debris. Riverbanks were strewn with precious belongings like photographs, heirlooms, clothing and more.

With emergency officials, I had been warning Vermonters for days to prepare for the impending storm that was moving up the Atlantic seaboard toward New England, advising them to prepare for the worst but hope for the best. Vermonters have survived enough blizzards, ice storm and flooding to take weather warnings seriously, and for the most part we all stocked up on food and water, batteries, flashlights and transistor radios.

As governor, I was hoping for the best.

On the afternoon of Aug. 28, as we all waited to see what Irene would deliver, I received my first look at the reality headed Vermont's way. My brother Jeff texted to my cell phone a photograph of a washed-out dirt road near our family home in Putney, where a small brook now resembled a river. Although I was shocked at the high water level of that brook, I held out hope the storm would veer off toward the Atlantic, doing minimal damage.

Shortly after that, Jeff sent more photos, these of downtown Brattleboro, where the Whetstone Brook buried Sam's Army & Navy store, the Latchis Theater and all of Flat Street in raging water and mud. Imagining that little brook transforming into such a menacing force was shocking. I knew then that we were in deep trouble.

A few hours later, just after midnight, I received a call that we needed to evacuate the Waterbury state office complex, the Vermont State Hospital and our Emergency Management center. I realized that despite hopes for the best, Irene was giving us her worst.

When the winds died down and the rain stopped the next morning, National Guard General Michael Dubie and I climbed aboard a Guard helicopter and headed out to survey the damage. Nothing could have prepared me for the destruction below.

Long stretches of Route 107 along the White River were gone – not just broken up or potholed, but this major thoroughfare was now a riverbed. Homes along riverbanks were broken into piles of lumber, glass and furniture. Cars and trucks were partially submerged in sandbars. One large round bale of hay, still wrapped in its white plastic jacket, was lodged between two rocks along the Mad River outside Moretown. Calls for everything from cots to generators to medical supplies were coming in to my office and Vermont Emergency Management from all over the state.

Touching down in communities large and small, General Dubie and I were devastated by what we saw and heard. Tearful Vermonters had seen their homes washed downstream in Pittsfield, Rochester and West Windsor; businesses washed away in Wilmington, Waitsfield and Wardsboro; Vermonters lost their lives in Mendon and Ludlow. Yet in every tragedy and heartbreaking loss, victims were universally grateful for the love and caring from fellow Vermonters.

Every morning I was back up in the chopper heading to stricken parts of the state. Communities that had been isolated were opening up to limited traffic, power to the 70,000 homes and businesses left in the dark by Irene were gradually getting light, schools were resuming (in some cases children were walking miles to catch a bus or a lift from someone who could reach the school by automobile), and stores, restaurants and inns were doing their best to convince customers they were open for business.

But something far more uplifting was also happening. People kept coming out of their damaged homes carrying shovels and heading elsewhere to help those who had been harder hit. Vermonters were washing and folding clothes to donate to strangers who lost everything. People kept flooding into damaged towns with food and equipment, offering any assistance. President Obama called to offer his help. My fellow Governors sent National Guard units from Virginia, Maine and West Virginia who expected to find shell-shocked storm victims, but instead received a warm welcome from Vermonters already digging out and stacking debris from the storm, trying to get their lives back in some order before the coming winter season.

In Jamaica and Hancock, volunteers staffed a make-shift donation center overflowing with tables of clothing, kitchen utensils and other essentials in the town halls. In Moretown, a woman whose home was partially covered in mud described the joy she felt when hundreds of strangers knocked on the door and asked, "How can I help?" In Northfield, hundreds of cadets from Norwich University joined fellow Vermonters gutting damaged homes around Water Street. In Waterbury, 500 volunteers turned out to help clean up damaged homes and businesses downtown. In 45 towns, strangers showed up to help strangers.

Vermont suffered a tremendous blow from Tropical Storm Irene. Many of the stories were told by people in tears, Vermonters who lost so much that they loved. I will never forget the lives lost in the storm, or the heartbreaking funerals I attended with the friends and families of the good people who became the ultimate victims of Irene.

But I am proudest of what we reaffirmed about ourselves in this historic disaster. Vermonters are strong in heart and spirit. We put the well-being of our neighbors ahead of our own. We don't give up and we don't back down. Irene did her best to deliver a knockout blow to our state, but Vermonters and this community are stronger today than on Aug. 28 when that little brook in Putney briefly became a river.

Together we will rebuild our state better than the way Irene found us. And we will be stronger for it.

GOVERNOR PETER SHUMLIN

Sue Flewelling, the Rochester cemetery caretaker, contemplates a casket washed from its resting place by Irene.

THANKSGIVING

Susan Mordecai, a teacher at Clarendon Elementary School, lost her home in Plymouth during Tropical Storm Irene. She wrote these words on Thanksgiving Day.

I am thankful for water, the pond that draws us together, the wellspring of words.

I am thankful for water, the rivers that have ripped us open only so that we find that seamless continuity.

I am thankful for the water that fills my sink, and for my hands that find comfort beneath the frictionless foam.

I am thankful for water, for the cup of tea waiting patiently for me, loyal friend.

All that remains of Susan Mordecai's home in Plymouth.

Susan Mordecai sent her damaged Bose system to the company; they sent her a new one.

A couple inspects the destruction at M's RV on Route 12 south of Montpelier Monday morning after Irene.

A vintage Austin Healy at Extra Room Storage by the Winooski River in Middlesex.

A MIGHTY STORM

Adjectives like epic and historic seem hardly adequate to describe the worst weather event in 84 years that arrived at Vermont's borders while most people were still asleep on August 28, 2011. There had been warnings of the storm's power as it pummeled states to the south of Vermont. Residents had done as advised – filled the gas tank, loaded up on water and non-perishables, candles and batteries. But the average person associates gale-force winds with hurricanes. Irene had already been downgraded from hurricane to tropical storm status before it reached Vermont. Rain? Yes, there would be rain. Flooding was expected. Parts of the state had been through destructive floods twice already in 2011. Hopefully, Irene would be no worse.

As it turned out, Vermont's streams and rivers, even many of the state's most placid brooks, could not hold the torrent of water, as much as eight inches in a few hours, that poured relentlessly onto already sodden ground. "I consider it a missile," Randolph Fire Chief Ray Colette said of the gushing water that blasted through the Lincoln Bridge, leaving a 15-foot gap. Few Vermonters had experienced anything like it.

Vermont had been primed for disaster. It was an especially snowy winter, with up to 200 inches of snow recorded in some locations. Winter was followed by an exceptionally wet spring – generally three to five inches above the average monthly total, setting records in March, April and May. Those rains had brought severe flooding to Lake Champlain, which reached a record level of 103.20 feet on May 6, 2011, breaking the previous record set in 1869 and damaging 500 homes. The lake remained above flood stage for two months.

And along the Winooski River, spring flooding had taken a heavy toll as swollen streams and rivers tore through central Vermont on May 26 and 27, swamping basements in Montpelier, flooding the newsroom and the pressroom for the Barre-Montpelier Times Argus, and pushing tons of silt into central Vermont homes and businesses. Indeed, as spring ended, Essex, Franklin, Grand Isle, Lamoille, Chittenden, Addison, Orleans and Washington counties were each so damaged from flooding that they qualified for federal disaster relief; many residents faced long months of rebuilding and refinancing.

Vermont had a relatively dry summer but in mid-August, from the 15th to 16th, the state got drenched again. With precipitation totals of more than two inches in central and eastern Vermont and intermittent rain over the next two weeks, Vermont was essentially saturated.

Then, Tropical Storm Irene arrived with its own record-setting rainfall, between 3.2 and 8.15 inches depending on locale, shattering records dating back to the summers of 1949, 1950 and 1971. The rain itself didn't seem that terrifying but, as meteorologist Chris Bouchard of the Fairbanks Museum and Planetarium explains, each individual drop was quite large. The storm, which had swept up the Eastern Seaboard dumping and collecting water all along its route, was like "an elongated bull's eye along the eastern side of the Green Mountains, with the worst precipitation falling along the western side of the storm's circulation pattern. It moved north-northeast right up the Connecticut River Valley," Bouchard says, resulting in "the eastern slopes of the Green Mountains getting the brunt of the rainfall."

It was a lesson in the destructive power of water unlike any seen since the flood of 1927. Within hours, from Wilmington to Waterbury, dozens of towns became islands, and within those island communities countless residents were further isolated from their neighbors, marooned by floodwaters, their homes destroyed or inundated with mud, power lines down, lives and possessions lost. The most isolated communities – those that couldn't be reached by outside roads — included Bennington, Wilmington, Stratton, Cavendish, Chester, Granville, Killington, Mendon, Middletown Springs and Stratton. While some were quickly reconnected, for other communities, the wait for outside help was days in coming.

Four people died in the flood, at least 1,400 homes and businesses were destroyed or severely damaged, 70,000 homes were without electricity, more than 500 miles of roads including sections of routes 7, 4, 9 and 100 were closed, and roughly 200 bridges wrecked or undermined, so much so that state and local officials were overwhelmed by emergencies. Indeed, while the communities of East Montpelier, Plainfield, Marshfield and Cabot, which had sustained thousands of dollars in damage from spring flooding, fared better during Tropical Storm Irene, Waterbury was not so fortunate.

Floodwaters from the Winooski River inundated the state's emergency command center, forcing the emergency workers to evacuate and relocate to Burlington. A similar occurrence happened in Rutland Town, where the State Police barracks was flooded.

Rescues were many – by all-terrain vehicle, kayak, and swift-water teams that were dispatched all over the state – even for one woman in labor, and more than 700 people took refuge in shelters.

But something else happened in the hours and days, weeks and months after Tropical Storm Irene ravaged whole swaths of Vermont, something quite extraordinary. While the storm caused at least $125 million in property damage, another roughly $100 million to repair state roads after federal disaster aid, and perhaps millions more to rebuild town and private roads, in devastated town after town, a more important story emerged – that of neighbor helping neighbor, of resilience and ingenuity, hard work and immeasurable generosity. Again, from the Deerfield River Valley to Lake Champlain, from south to north and east to west, not only did the people in these tiny outposts and isolated communities work together to rescue the stranded and begin rebuilding roads, salvaging what they could from the debris, but they rediscovered bonds of strength and resiliency that lie within all of us. The lessons are many, and there are many yet to be learned, but in rebuilding their state and doing so with little whining or bitterness, Vermonters proved that the Green Mountain State is still a place our ancestors might recognize, a place where challenges are met with hard work and creativity rather than passed on to someone else to fix. The future always poses uncertainty and for those who suffered the most from Irene, loss will be part of that future. But, as we continue to learn, together we are Vermont Strong.

This house in Bethel survived the '27 flood, but not Irene in '11.

THE POWER OF WATER

The name Irene comes from the Greek word meaning peace, but Tropical Storm Irene was far from peaceful. Every river town had a story to tell about its fury. Vermont's topography and historic settlement patterns, in which towns grew up along streams and rivers, contributed to the problem. Even gentle brooks swelled in a remarkably short period of time due to the intensity of the rainfall, and with the swollen waters came unpredictable and often random damage to 82 towns and cities. For those following the storm, it was like watching a sweet friend turn relentless enemy as the rain arrived in Vermont's southern extreme, where the pretty town of Wilmington was among the first to feel the brunt.

Quickly, the village of about 100 was cut off from the state highway system as a chest-high sluice of water and debris scoured 19th century-era structures in the town center. Buildings disappeared in the deluge; the concrete pad for a home on Route 9 remained while the house, or what was left of it, could be seen floating in nearby Lake Whitingham along with a dozen or so propane tanks.

Town Clerk Susie Haughwout and a cadre of trusty friends spent hours using wheeled office chairs to move hundreds of pounds of town records, valuable maps and documents to the second floor while outside the Town Office windows a branch of the Deerfield River swelled and roiled. Haughwout finally left the town office as the river came rushing in, only to find her car inundated by floodwaters. The adjacent town police department had already been abandoned.

(top) The town of Wilmington, (center) including Town Clerk Susie Haughwout, and (bottom) Dot's Diner, was hit hard by Irene.

RIVERSIDE VERMONT

The picture postcard of Vermont often shows a sweet and tidy village with its clapboard and stone buildings hugging a bucolic river or stream; this is true too of many of the state's historic downtowns, their old brick buildings built near or even around a waterway. Think Brandon or Waterbury or Wilmington. That combination of man in consort with nature even in urban centers is not only attractive to residents of Vermont, but it has long attracted tourists to Vermont. Indeed, since the advent of the train and automobile, tourism has played a role in Vermont's settlement patterns, patterns that while placing many of these gathering places on the National Register of Historic Buildings also proved hazardous during Tropical Storm Irene.

Dona Brown, a history professor at the University of Vermont, says the earliest Vermonters did not build right along the rivers. While the Abenaki people who lived here before European settlers used Vermont's waterways for transportation and food, their settlements were often slightly above water in places that gave both a clear view as well as distance from flooding. The first settlers too, primarily English immigrants, tended to build higher up on hillsides for the most practical of reasons – the valleys of Vermont in the 18th Century were still quite marshy. The beaver hadn't been destroyed yet; nor had vast tracts of valley floor been drained.

These early settlers did not make their homes on the ridgelines either, but rather in protected areas along terraced or rolling hills, especially ones located just above wide river valleys with fertile valley floors. Crops might be grown in the valleys and animals grazed there, but the little towns and first hamlets were safely above flood levels.

By the 19th century, however, residents began building a variety of water-powered mills and small industries along the state's plentiful rivers. Still, Vermont saw very little industrialization before the Civil War, Brown says, and what there was tended to be widespread rather than organized in a few pockets around the state. Distances between settlements remained great and travel by horse or on foot was tedious. The more independent these small settlements could be the more successful they were; those that grew into villages had within them furniture makers, blacksmiths, tanners, tailors, farmers and craftspeople of all sorts.

As these enclaves became more successful and the small industries fueled by waterpower grew, more homes, as well as churches, schools and other gathering places, grew up around these riverside communities. It was during this time, around the middle of the 19th century, that the distribution of people in Vermont began to go through a major change.

Vermont had grown quickly during the early stages of settlement from 1791 to 1850 but population growth remained stagnant for the next hundred years. Others would call that statistic stability. Regardless, the fact of the matter is that the same number of people essentially lived in Vermont during those hundred years, but where they lived dramatically changed as people moved from farming communities to the cities and more established towns for work, often to villages that had grown up around rivers and streams.

At first, the migration was primarily women but later immigrants from Canada and Europe populated river towns like Windsor, Woodstock, Brattleboro, Springfield and St. Johnsbury. Indeed, around the turn of the 20th century, a scattering of industries located along the White River earned a section of Bethel and Stockbridge the nickname Little Detroit. Flooding during the historic Hurricane of 1927, the worst natural disaster to strike Vermont prior to Tropical Storm Irene and one with many times more deaths than in 2011, wiped out the factories of Little Detroit. While a few were rebuilt, the Great

Depression finished the job. Little Detroit was located near where Route 107 was demolished by floodwaters in Irene.

The second factor contributing to the development of settlements along waterways – or their expansion – was the introduction of the train. Not only did train service allow transportation of goods in and out of communities, but it also provided a means for tourists to come to these scenic villages. The village centers grew and the former settlement centers on the hillsides became the outskirts of town.

This pattern – the original town often now given the moniker "center" to its place name –was quite prevalent. Examples, says Brown, can be found in places like Randolph with its original settlement now called Randolph Center, up the hill. There, two branches of the White River provided power and by 1859, the village boasted three gristmills; the arrival of the railroad brought prosperity to the town and with that prosperity came the building of two of the town's finest examples of architecture, the Randolph Railroad Depot and Kimball Public Library. Fortunately, during Irene, while some buildings just yards away from the library were flooded, its location just uphill from the White River protected it from harm.

Not so Wilmington and Waterbury, Brandon and so many other iconic village centers.

"Poor Waterbury," Brown says, silent for a moment as she pictures the damage to so many historic buildings in this central Vermont community, including the State Office complex, still unusable months after the flood.

"Waterbury Center is on high ground," she says. "What we think of as Waterbury is right where the railroad went through." Indeed, according to its town history, "the railroad … contributed to the relocation of the center of local activity from Waterbury Center to Waterbury Village." Waterbury Village was hard hit in the 1927 flood; Waterbury, Connecticut residents sent $10,000 to Waterbury, Vermont, to replace books destroyed in the flood.

These villages and towns "look good to us now," Brown says, "but they were the 19th century equivalent of a strip mall."

The next factor influencing settlement and development patterns comes with the next major development in transportation, the automobile, and with it more tourists. In the 1890s, says Brown, there was a nationwide move to build scenic roads, the equivalent of state highways, in large part intended for tourists. Naturally, the easiest and least costly way to build roads through the mountains was to locate them along the edges of rivers and brooks, which, of course, made many roads vulnerable to flooding and difficult to fix.

Wilmington already had a small railroad station but the town's growth and its preservation as an iconic Vermont community is a result of its location along the scenic Deerfield River and because Route 9, which connects Bennington and Brattleboro and is close to the Massachusetts border, goes right through the town. Like other early tourist destinations, hotels and inns were built both within the village center and along its outskirts, often with the waterway as part of the enticement to the visitor.

Preserving these handsome waterside villages and towns became a priority as Vermont's tourism business expanded in the 20th century. In 1938, the Vermont Chamber of Commerce sponsored a conference entitled "Keeping 'Unspoiled Vermont' Unspoiled." Eight years later, in 1946, Vermont Life magazine was founded by the state to celebrate Vermont's unique character and promote tourism.

Like it or not, "what's allowed these towns to stay so picturesque was the automobile travel and the tourist trade," Brown says. Today, for many, further steps will need to be taken to preserve these communities and the cost for many will be great.

Just across the bridge at the intersection of Route 100 and 9, Dot's diner, a wood-framed building overlooking the river, was badly damaged. Built as a post office in 1832 and opened as a restaurant since 1935, Dot's was legendary for its berry-berry pancakes, chili and burgers but its role as a local gathering place was equally essential to the community. The building had been damaged in the 1927 flood; this one, however, did it in. Another favorite café, Beanheads, also suffered damage. Throughout the downtown, stores that defined the community were filled with muck, their contents ruined, their basements and first floors flooded; in less than a day, what had taken generations to build was made immeasurably vulnerable.

Ivana Taseva, 20, was working as a housekeeper at the Mount Snow ski area in Dover on a student visa. She became the first person in Vermont to die as a result of Irene. Taseva was in a car with her boyfriend and two other men when they came upon an area of road flooding. When the car began to be swept away by floodwaters, the two men were able to get to safe ground. Taseva's boyfriend was able to hold on to the car but she was swept away and drowned. From Mount Snow to Taseva's hometown far away, the question remained unanswered: how could a woman described universally as someone who made a room light up with happiness, a ray of sunshine in the blush of her youth, die so randomly?

By day's end, 13 homes here had been severely damaged and the town's commercial district was under water. Wilmington had the worst property damage in Vermont from Tropical Storm Irene, more than $13 million.

Town after town, it happened like that – the rain accumulating, some small flooding and then, in a matter of hours as sheets of water gauged their way down mountainsides, rivers swelled, surged over their banks, carried away trees, lawns and foundations, turned roads into quagmires and sent home after home, some more than 200 years old, down streams along with their owners' possessions. And for the most part, during that first day, Vermonters were powerless to do much about it.

While Wilmington's village center was going under water, Bennington and Brattleboro and small towns in between were also under attack. To the west of Wilmington in Brattleboro, the Whetstone Brook filled Flat Street and its historic buildings. Water lines on the exteriors of the town's classic brick structures illustrated the brook's 5-foot rise, while inside the destruction was monumental. The 73-year-old Art Deco Latchis Hotel and Theater was flooded, causing at least $500,000 in damage and the loss of the foliage season's income. The theater was constructed in 1938 as a "town within a town" and is listed on the National Register of Historic Buildings. It had been restored through community effort and fund-raising; by day's end, questions about its sustainability floated along with the muck that ruined a basement restaurant and closed the hotel down. Elsewhere along Flat Street, the Boys and Girls Club of Brattleboro was gutted, mud dumped where a dance floor had been. Nearby, Dottie's Discount Foods and the Brattleboro Hospice Thrift Store were a mess.

The Whetstone also flooded the Glen Park and Mountain Home trailer parks, easy pickings due to their low, flat locations, and damaged the Cooke Road Bridge. Tim Hamilton's three-generation sawmill and sugaring operations were badly damaged.

In Newfane, a town of 1700, more than 150 people were stranded from home, about 30 of them stuck in their cars as seven bridges washed out. A gristmill built in 1838 was turned into kindling.

Just east of Bennington, a bridge linking the community to the town of Woodford collapsed - not unusual, except the collapse also carried away the pipe that carried Bennington's water supply in from the Woodford filtration plant. The intake to the plant was also submerged, forcing the town to jerry-rig alternative water sources for a few days.

Elsewhere, Barbara Bermudez had parked her blue Plymouth Acclaim in a temporary garage to protect it from the expected wind from Irene. The car, and 30 feet of land behind her house, were washed away by the Roaring Branch - and the car gained national attention when a bystander captured it on video, bobbing down the river through Bennington.

"Then I saw it on TV. I thought, 'That's my car.' … At first, it's kinda funny. (The car) looked so pretty. It didn't look banged up. It looked good," she said. The loss wasn't covered by insurance, but Bermudez wasn't too worried. "Compared to what other people suffered, I'm not that upset about it."

SAVING HISTORY

Paul Bruhn, executive director of The Preservation Trust of Vermont, watched as Tropical Storm Irene swept through Vermont, scouring the foundations of notable old buildings and pummeling covered bridges that his organization, Vermont communities and countless benefactors had restored and protected over Vermont's long history.

Among the many thoughts going through his mind was relief at what had been saved but that feeling was tempered by what had been lost. As he looked to the future, he saw an even greater dilemma, how to protect and preserve not just individual buildings but groups of historic structures that together tell a deeper story than any individual relic could. As he said in an interview with the Associated Press about the need to look at historic districts as a collective, "One of the things that's wonderful about Vermont and Vermont's historic resources is each of them is important individually -- but it's the collection that really makes a place special. If you wiped it out, it would be like losing your front teeth."

His organization and many Vermont towns faced a daunting future: more than 700 buildings of historic value had been damaged by flood waters. Yet, within a day of the damage being broadcast around Vermont and to the outside world, funds were pouring into organizations like Bruhn's. More, of course, would be needed but the initial outpouring buoyed people far and near and showed that these vestiges of Vermont's past weren't just important to Vermonters and to historians but were also treasured by the general public. Many people who sent in money and well-wishes were responding to a video posted on YouTube showing the Bartonsville Bridge, built in 1870 and listed on the National Register of Historic Places, rather gracefully float down the Williams River before breaking apart.

Whetstone Brook overflows into downtown Brattleboro.

Susan Harmond's video of the Bartonsville Bridge's demise and the lamentations of those watching it demonstrated graphically how much these bridges mean to people. Another privately owned covered bridge in Pittsfield was dismantled by the storm waters; the Taftsville and Quechee covered bridges had substantial damage as did one of three covered bridges over Cox Brook in Northfield Falls. In all, Vermont has about 100 covered bridges.

Bruhn had seen videos and still photographs of the damage to Wilmington but was still unprepared for the havoc. Rushing water had overpowered the center of the downtown, moved buildings around and caused

substantial structural damage to the town offices, Dot's Diner and many other historic buildings. Even so, he said, here and throughout the state, while there was no end to the challenges, "most of the buildings in village centers and downtowns are very salvageable, if there's the will and the resources to do it. Many are significantly water-damaged but are structurally sound."

That's the good news. The bad news is in that phrase "if there's the will and the resources."

In a survey of historical buildings in 30 communities, Bruhn and other conservationists found along with the 700 historic buildings with structural damage located within Vermont downtown districts and village centers, another 300 to 400 individual buildings were also impacted. Waterbury alone had 183 individual buildings of historic merit that were affected.

But Vermont and its historic resources hold a special place in the hearts of many. People like Charity Clark, who used to work for former Governor Howard Dean and is now a New York lawyer, watched the destruction and felt she had to do something. She launched a Facebook page that raised money for rebuilding bridges and buildings. Some Wall Street brokers who also have a band put on a fundraiser. Another woman ran in a marathon to raise money to rebuild Vermont's historic structures.

These efforts together garnered more than $30,000 while Newman's Own company donated another $30,000; the Walter Cerf Fund at the Vermont Community Foundation raised another $20,000 and another $10,000 came from the Alma Gibbs Donchian Foundation of Castleton – all of that unsolicited.

The plan, at least immediately after Irene, was to divide the money fairly evenly between rebuilding and restoring Vermont's covered bridges, emergency repairs to threatened structures; and grants to support downtowns and village gathering centers.

"We can't abandon these places," Bruhn said.

Upper Covered Bridge over the Cox Brook in Northfield had a tree thrust entirely through it.

DO NOT
PARK
FOR HOTEL
GUESTS ONLY

Brattleboro's downtown, already reeling from a major fire earlier this year, was inundated.

In Bennington, where plazas and streets were described as a churning sea of muck, volunteer and town work crews showed up even as the rain was still falling; they rescued a couple stranded in the Hampton Inn. "When everyone realized we had a baby, they put us in a vehicle out of the rain and took us to the shelter" at Mount Anthony Union High School, said Teresa Bryanton of British Columbia. Throughout Sunday, workers used an inflatable raft and rowboats to rescue people, about 170 of whom were housed at the middle school in town.

"There wasn't much we could do to stop what was happening, but I believe that these volunteers prevented loss of life," Bennington Town Manager Stuart Hurd said the next day.

North of Wilmington, Wardsboro was hard hit. At least five homes were destroyed, including the home rented by Jackie Bedard, the town clerk; she lost all her possessions. A home owned by Kevin Coyne of Connecticut fell into the South Wardsboro Brook. Several bridges were badly damaged. The town of 850 was without power for five days. Route 100 had more than a dozen washouts, making it impassable. Norman Bills, a 42-year-old mail carrier, marveled at the storm's ferocity, turning a brook that just days previously was so shallow kids could hardly find a place to swim into an unrecognizable beast that tore off his garage and dining room and heaved his wood-burning stove downriver. He feared the house, which had belonged to his grandfather, was beyond fixing.

While Randolph Fire Chief Ray Colette had compared the floodwaters to a missile, Wardsboro's emergency coordinator Duane Tompkins likened the torrent to a tsunami, describing how a 15-foot wall of water took out a beaver pond, creating a 90-foot wave that annihilated parts of town. He said of the 99 roads in Wardsboro, 85 percent had some damage. A half mile of Gilfeather Road was one of many town roads destroyed by flooding. But here, as elsewhere, volunteers like Mike Babbitt, who removed trees blocking roads and rivers, came by the dozens to help. A team of more than 20 on ATVs made the rounds to all those who were isolated in storm-ravaged pockets of town.

Here also, Tompkins struggled with a question asked in town after town: how to begin fixing roads and restoring electricity and then rebuild homes and businesses when the roads themselves were so dismantled that equipment couldn't get in? The answer in Wardsboro, as elsewhere, came intrinsically from the people themselves as locals with equipment jumped into rivers with their backhoes and excavators, beginning the process of restoring infrastructure. But as Bills predicted as early as nightfall on August 28, the slog back to normalcy would be long and hard.

The water isolated homes and people from roads, bridges and any semblance of normalcy.

Neighboring Jamaica was also devastated as the Bald Mountain Brook and its tributaries tore through the little town of 952, literally pulling away roads, yards and foundations and sending homes down the river like rafts. In a few hours, the town center became isolated, islands within islands as residents on one side of the bridge through town were cut off from residents on the other. The fire department was separated from the town center by a huge gap in Route 100 where a bridge had been. In total, 11 homes in Jamaica had more than 50 percent damage and 94 were seriously damaged. Beyond that, the town's two major rural roads, the West Jamaica Road and Pikes Falls Road, were mere remnants of their former selves, with huge stretches shattered, chasms everywhere, and people stranded far and wide.

Meanwhile, with that huge eye of the storm settled over Vermont, the devastation along Vermont's eastern border with the Connecticut River quickly reached crisis proportions. A litany of loss was being

PARROT RESCUE AND THE GOODNESS OF THE GUARD

Published in the Rutland Herald and Times Argus on Nov. 7, 2011
By YVONNE DALEY

The T-shirt says it all. On the front, simply the words Jamaica, Vermont. On the back, an excavator in the river and the words, "Fix it now. Apologize later."

Quick action and collaborative efforts, not to mention a strong dose of independent thinking and a dollop of good fortune, saved the village of Jamaica from greater devastation when Tropical Storm Irene turned the Bald Mountain Brook and its tributaries from familiar, meandering streams into monsters of destruction.

Six homes simply gone and others rearranged into something that resembles a structure but will take a lot of time and money before it can be lived in again; acre upon acre of land churned up and deposited elsewhere; roads hacked into frayed segments, one disconnected by a 50-foot chasm – that was the story of Jamaica, a town of 952 in south-central Vermont, one of those hit hardest by the Irene.

Since then, dozens of roads through town have been repaired or rebuilt, although old Route 8 is still out as are several small roads and bridges in outlying areas. But, how the reconstructed roads will hold up through winter and spring remains to be seen.

"Mud season's going to be fun," says Paul Fraser, the town's emergency coordinator who retired here 14 years ago after a 20-year career with the Air Force where he was a psychotherapist specializing in terrorism and hostage negotiation. Fraser, also a selectman, says the National Guard, Agency of Transportation and private contractors have done an amazing job in a short period of time, but there may not be time to pave roads before winter.

Although most residents whose homes were wrecked have found temporary housing, qualms about how much support they will receive from FEMA and concerns about mortgages and taxes continue, especially for those who have no land left upon which to rebuild. Beyond that, Fraser worries about the long-term emotional impacts.

"They haven't had time to grieve the situation; they're still living the crisis. They can't move on," Fraser said the day after the town held its first tax abatement meeting, one story of loss after another.

"I'm just living from one uncertainty to another," says Tracy Payne, who lost her three-story home built in the 1940s, most of the land it was built upon, and her possessions.

Quick action

Bad as it was, Fraser says it could have been worse. When a mobile home and considerable debris from upstream piled under the bridge near the center of town across Route 100, water rose quickly and began flooding to either side, threatening the town's small business center. Fortunately, the bridge collapsed and the clog went with it.

Unfortunately, it took several weeks to get a temporary bridge installed, one of dozens of breaks in Route 100 in this part of Vermont.

But while most village businesses were spared, homes on either side of the commercial district were not. The river swiped a kitchen off the back of one home on Factory Street and sheared away neighboring backyards, foundations and land. It was far worse on the other side of the commercial district, on Water Street.

Andy Coyne, the town's health officer, watched as his neighborhood was erased, home after home undermined, then swept away into the raging river. Somehow, the house he and his wife called Graceland – her first name is Grace -- was spared.

"I haven't been right since," Coyne said, conceding he felt some survivor's guilt. "You can't be relieved that your house was spared, yet you are, and we feel so bad. It's all around us."

Fix it, apologize later
It didn't take resident Wesley Ameden and his construction crew long to realize not only that the bridge outage posed a danger, but also that water rushing under and around it was eating away at properties and

foundations. Ameden blocked the bridge to keep people away, then went into the river with an excavator to divert the river back to where it had come from, perhaps saving other structures.

After that, "in eight or 10 hours, they built a road that essentially became Routes 30 and 100," says Fraser. "Without that, no one was moving north." The new road was built where the four lost homes and their properties once were.

The Command Center
Seven years ago, when Ed and Jennifer Dorta-Duque moved from Washington, D.C., to own and operate the Three Mountains Inn in the center of town, they put in a generator and Ed, who is a volunteer fireman, agreed to let the inn be used as a command center in case of emergency. He was thinking a three-day snowstorm. In Irene, it also became one of three shelters in town.

Meetings were held in the inn's homey great room or one of several cozy dining rooms. The couple housed the stranded and fed them along with emergency volunteers, including members of the Green Mountain Club who came to restore trails in Jamaica State Park and ended up mucking out flooded basements because the park was closed to the public.

In all, they housed 40 or 50 people over the first several weeks after the flood, all for free. Ed cooked. And it was good.

Meanwhile, dozens of residents took part in the rescue and restoration process. Becky Tolbert and Duffy Chapin organized donations and distributed food and clothing from the Jamaica Community Church.

Drew Hazelton took a week off from work at Rescue, Inc. in Brattleboro, where his job includes training new EMTs and communication between emergency response teams, to organize a team of residents who scoured the town on all-terrain vehicles, checking on residents who were marooned.

One of the more entertaining stories involves road commissioner Brian Chapin and selectman Stewart Barker, also a fire warden, who arrived at a particularly damaged part of the West Jamaica Road, saw an excavator nearby, found the key, used it to fix the road, then returned the excavator and put the key back in its hidey-place.

Resilience is a requirement for living on the back roads here and most of the stranded stayed home, but there were plenty of people who needed checking on or supplies delivered.

In all, 34 people, four dogs, three cats and one parrot were rescued by ATV.

A favorite story in town is that Toby Schwartz, who owns the parrot with her husband Hank, asked the ATV driver to slow down a few times, whereupon the parrot, named Gravy, took up the command, screeching "Slow down," for the two and a half hour ATV ride on a makeshift trail through the woods.

Not true, says Hank Schwartz; it was his wife who screamed as they rode through the mud and muck. Gravy, wrapped carefully in a blanket so he could still see, just laughed the whole way.

Three days after Irene, the town suffered a microburst, particularly damaging in an isolated area called Rawsonville. Massive amounts of rain came down, more roads flooded, a mud slide hit a home and forced one man into the shelter; other people were rescued from rapidly rising water. But on-the-job training helped volunteers respond quickly and efficiently.

Fraser had been finalizing a town emergency management plan before the storm, in part based on participation in more crisis situations than he likes to recall. He says he's never encountered a smoother operation.

"Jennifer (Dorta-Duque) was my deputy and took over the command post when I couldn't be there. Kristi (Ameden) has a remarkable knowledge of everyone's homes in town. She had an incredible presence for a young person. People came in and did what needed to be done. I just got out of the way," he says.

But Karen Ameden, holding up the draft emergency plan, says it was Fraser's organizational skills that provided the structure for volunteer efforts to work. "It was like a finely tuned machine," Ameden says.

The General Store
Ameden and husband Dale own K&D's Jamaica General Store where the T-shirts with local attitude are on sale. In ordinary times, the store is the community clearinghouse where people pass along the information of the day, deliver and receive messages, commiserate. During and after Irene, it was the secondary command center, essential for supplies and information on disaster relief.

"I came here to find out what I was doing," Fraser jokes. A yellow T-shirt in the window tells a part of the story. It's a gift from the #131 Engineer Company of the Vermont National Guard who spent several weeks here rebuilding Pikes Falls Road. Fraser says the road simply wouldn't be there if it weren't for the Guard.

Guard members stopped here often for food and supplies. The Amedens wouldn't take their money. Karen Ameden had heard that some Guard members were only making $17 a day. They were there to help the town; it was the least she and her husband could do to feed them.

Besides, she adds, most of them would toss their money in the Irene collection jars when she refused it.

Resilience is a requirement for living on the back roads here...

Reconstruction – of homes and the riverbed – begins along Bald Mountain Brook in Jamaica.

OPPOSITES ATTRACT
Published in the Rutland Herald and Times Argus on Nov. 7, 2011
By YVONNE DALEY

Paul Fraser and Greg Joly have lived in Jamaica for years but were essentially strangers until Tropical Storm Irene introduced them to one another.

Unlike the tidy fringe of clipped white hair on Fraser's head, Joly's brown hair reaches past his shoulders; and while Fraser wears the customary attire of jeans and ball cap, Joly sports an Amish-style straw hat and front-flap pants for comfort, durability and to keep the cops from hassling him over his long hair.

Fraser is joking when he calls himself a paramilitary fascist pig, but after a long career in the Air Force – from his days in Thailand during the Vietnam War to work as a military psychotherapist and member of the National Ski Patrol – Fraser has stuck close to conservative views.

He moved to Jamaica 14 years ago to ski and golf, but found he couldn't just retire. He is both a selectman and the town's emergency coordinator. His house, built in 1830, is close to town. He enjoys his creature comforts.

Joly and his wife Mary Diaz, live off the grid and deep in the woods off West Jamaica Road in a compact cabin built from logs milled from their property and fitted together using only hand tools. A researcher, annotator, poet and printer, Joly has made almost everything in their house.

While Diaz works as director of special education at Burr and Burton Academy, Joly prints chapbooks and handsome notes on a 1894 letterpress printer and writes in what he calls his "writer's block," an 8-by-10-foot wooden structure he built and outfitted with a desk, his grandfather's typewriter, a small woodstove and walls of books.

Joly moved to the area 20 years ago in part because political activist Scott Nearing had lived nearby when he left New York City in 1932. Nearing had been an economics professor but lost his teaching position over his political views – he was a Socialist, pacifist and advocate for living simply.

In Vermont, Nearing and his wife Helen raised organic vegetables and produced maple syrup on their land at the foot of Stratton Mountain. Their many books, including "Living the Good Life" and "The Maple Book," inspired several back-to-the-land movements. Joly is currently annotating Nearing's books, a formidable task in and of itself, and serves on the board of the Good Life Center in Harborside, Me., where the Nearings spent their last years.

Joly measures his carbon footprint. He shoveled the 1,200-foot driveway to his house until a few years ago when he bought a snowblower. By way of contrast, while

Fraser often walks to work, he says, "My idea of camping is having to walk across the street to McDonald's."

Of course, the two men had seen each other many times in the years they've both lived in Jamaica, but they had rarely if ever spoken until Joly reported for duty at the post-Irene command center Fraser had established at the Three Mountains Inn in the center of town. It soon became apparent that Joly's talents and familiarity with remote areas of Jamaica could come in handy.

Over the course of three or four days, Joly walked 60 miles of Jamaica's back country, trekking across mud, through battered woods and over boulder-strewn ravines, checking on residents and recording the condition of every property he visited. He contacted homeowners far and wide – about a third of properties in Jamaica are second homes or camps -- to report on their condition. And he provided all this information to the town in an orderly report, saving immeasurable time and effort, especially given that roads in the areas he traversed were then nonexistent.

Turns out the two men do have a few things in common. Each has a fascination with the ways in which something as seemingly innocuous as water had rearranged their town, with learning why some properties were damaged while others went unscathed. They also love the workings of machinery – watching tandem rock crushers turn boulders into gravel or men

with nicknames like Bozo and Bozo Junior put the river back where it was supposed to be.

"It wasn't a flood that we had. It was a geological event," Joly observed as they drove on a road that had been a river for three weeks and observed how the river had rearranged the landscape.

"I have so much respect for him," Fraser says, not only referring to Joly's contributions to the response effort, but also what he has built in Jamaica's woods. It's doubtful he would have stepped into Joly's compact house or seen the couple's tidy garden if not for Irene.

As they check on the progress of improvements, they tell the story of finding a house that had been demolished, then washed away in the storm. All that remained was the pump house, what looked to be some flooring, and 50 or 60 feet away from where it once anchored the house, the foundation, seemingly whole.

"Literally, a river runs through it," Joly said and Fraser nodded.

When they got out to explore, they discovered a refrigerator caught in the debris pile farther downstream, inside a single soda. They left it for the archaeologists.

recorded in White River Junction, Saxtons River and Bellows Falls. One of the most dramatic videos seen internationally on YouTube the day of the storm showed the Bartonsville Covered Bridge spanning the Williams River in Rockingham as it was washed away. The lamentations of residents watching its demise were quite poignant, recorded for posterity in a manner and with tools unavailable to previous humans.

Fortunately, other tools were available, tools that had been put into place after previous floods in 1927 and 1938. Floodgates and dams along the Connecticut River operated as engineered and forward-thinking officials who opened them and sent water down the Connecticut River prior to and during the early stages of the storm undoubtedly reduced the extent of the damage. Still, the town of Hartford, which includes White River Junction, Quechee, Hartford, West Hartford and Wilder, had countless flood-related losses.

In White River Junction, Melvin and Damaris Hall had nearly completed renovations and an expansion to their catering company Tastes of Africa when floodwaters ravaged their new kitchen, causing so much damage that they had to relocate. In West Hartford, the public library on Route 14 was flooded to about 8 inches deep on the first floor, wrecking the entire children, teen and young adult's book section and causing serious damage to books on bottom shelves of the first floor.

The library had been built from a Sears kit in 1928 after the original library located across the street was destroyed in the 1927 flood. Residents from Hartford, Connecticut had sent money after the 1927 flood for the new building.

In White River Junction, employees and volunteers were able to rescue the entire collection of the Shultz Library during the early morning hours of August 28 with the sound of rising waters in the background and emergency lights blazing. Located in the historic Bridge Street firehouse on the edge of the White River, it contains a selection of contemporary graphic novels, rare gag cartoons and classic newspaper strips, and extensive holdings about cartooning, illustration and animation. The books were moved to the Telegraph Building a few blocks away where the only apparent damage was that the collection was a little jumbled.

Route 100, a 216-mile ribbon of asphalt that cuts through Vermont's backbone, is recognized as one of the Scenic Drives of America for obvious reasons: handsome old towns located in deep valleys, with scenic rivers flowing through them. The state's longest road, it slaloms along rocky riverbeds, climbs to astounding vistas and links the ski towns of Mount Snow, Okemo, Killington, Sugarbush, Stowe and Jay. But along Route 100 through the Green Mountains, there were no floodgates to open and the storm wreaked havoc, not just in Wilmington, Wardsboro and Jamaica, Londonderry and Weston but almost all the way north, decimating roads and washing away homes in Ludlow, Plymouth, Bridgewater, Pittsfield, Stockbridge, Rochester, Hancock, Granville, Moretown and Waterbury.

The town of Plymouth, for example, benefits from its location near Okemo Mountain and the presence of Echo, Amherst and Rescue lakes. This combination, along with the historic homestead of President Calvin Coolidge at Plymouth Notch, have long attracted tourists in all seasons and contributed to the town's settlement patterns near water.

The Roaring Brook that meandered past Susan Mordecai's house in Plymouth had hardly lived up to its name in the seven years she'd lived near it along Route 100, but the brook made up for that on August 28. Mordecai didn't sleep the night of the storm; the sound of rocks crashing down the river was terrifying. She'd never heard anything like it. Still, she had no intention of leaving; after all, the river was located a good 30 yards from her house and down a steep embankment. Finally, however, given warnings from town officials, she reluctantly drove away to a nearby shelter just moments before the river overflowed its banks, filling her house and swiping away the first floor, taking most of her worldly possessions, including heavy items like a refrigerator and snow blower, with it.

Mordecai's elderly neighbors, Dot and Roger Pingree, lost the home they had lived in since 1959 and the section of town named Pingree Flats — for Roger's ancestors — was essentially wiped out, stranding the Pingrees' son and daughter-in-law and many neighbors. Out-of-state homeowners offered their home to the Pingrees in the wake of the flood, but when Dot got a view of the damage the next day she cried at the destruction and conceded that rebuilding the home was nigh on impossible. Her geraniums and gladioli were gone, but she was grateful her chickens had survived.

At least four other people lost their homes in Plymouth and dozens more were damaged, particularly along the shores of Rescue, Echo and Amherst lakes, while not far away at Plymouth Notch, the Calvin Coolidge Homestead District and National Historic

PLYMOUTH DIGS OUT, STICKS TOGETHER
Published in the Rutland Herald and Times Argus on Sept. 21, 2011
By YVONNE DALEY

Susan Mordecai clambered over boulders and snagged branches, picking up pieces of her life strewn along Roaring Brook. There was the handle to the Delft mug she brought home from her visit to the Heineken Brewery in Amsterdam for her 21st birthday.

Shattered CDs, parts of her couch, chunks of favorite dishes, smashed photo frames and her Bose music system and, ironically enough, the saturated cover to a book she loved about living on less called "Plain and Simple" – these, some clothes, her car and a few pieces of furniture are all that remain of the 57-year-old teacher's worldly possessions.

There were mysteries floating down the river, scattered across the banks: where had the refrigerator gone? And the heavy snowblower? The river, normally flowing steadily roughly 30 yards away from her home and down a deep embankment, had filled with water and debris during the height of Tropical Storm Irene.

Mordecai heard the boulders crashing down, a sound that haunts her now, and escaped shortly before the water swallowed her home, crashing through walls,

As Halloween draws near, these Killington residents use a little humor to show defiance in the face of disaster.

taking everything in its path and leaving behind foot-deep waves of mud. The second floor is sound, almost untouched; the first demolished.

Mordecai, however, was not complaining.

"I've lost my rings, but I have my fingers. I've lost Michael's baby shoes but I have my son. I've lost my autographed books and photographs, but there are libraries I can visit, important people in my life, still alive," she said as she lugged the Bose player across the devastation.

"I'll send it to them; maybe they'll be able to fix it," the special education teacher at Clarendon Elementary School and part-time bartender at Okemo, said optimistically. "You know what? I'll be okay."

Then she trudged down the road to visit her neighbors, Roger Pingree and his wife Dot who had also been evacuated a week ago Sunday when the river overflowed its banks, tearing Route 100 apart and damaging the home they'd lived in since 1959.

Dot Pingree, 78, had planned to take her husband out to dinner to celebrate his 88th birthday Friday, a thank-you for his hard work tending their vegetable garden and the special care he'd given to her flowers, especially the gladiolus, her favorites. They're gone, along with the Mexican sunflowers Mordecai had given her at the beginning of the summer, and the shell beans Roger was waiting a few more days to pick.

Mordecai is currently staying with friends and has not yet returned to work. The Pingrees, along with their son Justus and his wife Michelle, are living in a neighbor's second home, a generosity among countless offers of help that have buoyed residents of one of the towns hardest hit by Irene. The younger Pingrees' home is unreachable by Frog City Road, another victim of the deluge.

At least four other people have lost their homes here and dozens more have been damaged, particularly along Roaring Brook and the shores of Rescue, Echo and Amherst lakes, while not far away at Plymouth Notch, the Calvin Coolidge Homestead District and National Historic Landmark were virtually unscathed.

Plymouth, a town of roughly 550 fulltime residents, was isolated from outside help for two to three days after the storm and then another four before it could be reached by anything other than four-wheel and emergency vehicles. Town officials said it would be particularly difficult to get a full assessment of the damage, given that 85 percent of town properties are second homes.

During the first few days, there were eight airdrops of food and water. The Vermont and Maine National Guard, the Salvation Army, Red Cross, state emergency workers and FEMA are all there now. But for most of the first week after Irene, it was neighbor helping neighbor.

"We were close-knit before; we're more so now," said Russ Tonkin, the town health officer and a licensed physician who helped with medical emergencies in the first few days after Irene. Since then, he and his wife Betsy, along with Justus Pingree and dozens of other volunteers have stood countless hours in the rain, directing traffic through hastily constructed and ingeniously built roads over and around Route 100, which in places now looks like a river-and rock-filled chasm.

Hope, humor and neighborliness have countered the losses. Residents have named the new road above the Route 100 washout "Rocky Road" and Mordecai jokes of putting up a sign outside her home advertising Plymouth Rocks for Sale. Residents Tina Verdrager and Margo Marrone cooked up a big community supper Tuesday night and arranged transportation for those stranded in the washout.

Willow Bascom, a volunteer helping the stranded and homeless at the Plymouth Town Office, pointed to tables covered with donated food and goods and page after page filled with names of people who had volunteered their services. She said residents were planning a Hurricane Hoe-down at the end of the month.

"We'll get through this the way we get through bad storms and sad times. We'll get through it together," she said. "We're Vermonters. We're resilient."

Landmark were virtually unscathed. Wilder House, the restaurant at the homestead, offered food and a gathering place to cut-off residents and visitors.

Plymouth, a town of roughly 550 full-time residents, was isolated from outside help for three days after the storm and then another four before it could be reached by anything other than four-wheel and emergency vehicles.

A second storm-related death added to the calamity. Kevin Davis, a 50-year-old Realtor and community supporter, was thought to be checking on his boat at Lake Rescue when he drowned at the height of the storm. Davis, the president of Mary W. Davis Real Estate, grew up in nearby Ludlow, itself hard-hit by the storm.

His death only added to the sorrow in Ludlow, where essentially every road in town had some damage. In the downtown area, the Shaw's supermarket located just off Main Street was filled with muck and debris, a total loss. Shaw's reopened in a tent in the parking lot once it had been cleared of silt about a week after the storm, but many businesses on the river side of Main Street, where the storm's damage seemed the worst, were badly flooded, including Sam's Steakhouse and Panarellos restaurant, both owned by Wally Sabotka of Rutland. Photos posted on Facebook the day after Tropical Storm Irene showed tablecloths in Sam's soaked in muddy water, furniture askew, the kitchen demolished and mud literally coating everything, but Sabotka vowed to rebuild.

In nearby Cavendish, flooding along the Black River caused a landslide that took out a huge section of Route 131, creating what was named "the Cavendish Canyon," 250 feet long and 52 feet deep, cutting off residents for more than two months. Mary McCallum, a librarian and Vermont Public Radio commentator, was not able to get off her hill — the road out was a 20-foot-chasm with rushing waters. If you got over that, there were many other washouts to navigate. A neighbor, Tim Mott, became a local hero, driving his ATV up and down Hardscrabble Road, a sizeable hill, helping people and ferrying them about. Mott brought his generator over one day so McCallum could get her computer going and meet a deadline.

The day before Irene, the small Rutland County town of Danby had celebrated its 250th anniversary. The Mount Tabor-Danby Historical Society had purchased a building once owned by the Nobel Prize-winning novelist Pearl Buck for $45,000 the previous

SHAW'S TURNS A TENT INTO A GROCERY STORE
Published in the Rutland Herald and Times Argus on Sept. 8, 2011
By KEVIN O'CONNOR

You can't buy anything alcoholic (no beer or wine), frozen (no ice cream) or custom cut (no four-fifths of a pound of ground round). Without scales, produce is sold by the piece rather than the pound. Without scanners, every item must be rung up on an old-fashioned cash register. Sound unpalatable? Shoppers here are eating it up.

Shaw's, the only supermarket within a half-hour radius of this tourist town once swam with locals stocking up before Tropical Storm Irene, only to sink under 3 feet of floodwater a week ago Sunday.

Cleaners soon realized it could take until Thanksgiving to reopen. And so, in what's believed to be a first for the 150-year-old New England chain, the store has pitched a tent in its Ludlow parking lot to sell household staples daily from 7 a.m. to 7 p.m.

"This community really requires a local grocery store," market director Darren Williams says, "and the company decided we needed to get something up sooner than later."

The Rain or Shine Tent and Events Co. of Randolph has erected a 3,000-square-foot white wedding canopy over a raised rubber floor. The canvas is a fifth the size of the waterlogged store behind it, so a company computer has whittled down its usual inventory of more than 20,000 items to the best-selling 700.

Step inside the new Route 103 location and you'll see a row of produce bins to the left, a dairy case to the right and six long shelves of canned, boxed and bagged goods in between.

Selection? Yes, you'll find Pop-Tarts (the nonperishable, no-heat treat ties with bottled water and batteries as the nation's top hurricane buy), but, no, don't look for frosted strawberry; just raspberry or brown sugar cinnamon.

Without electricity, the makeshift market's backup generators and batteries can power refrigerators but not freezers (hence milk but no ice cream), two cash registers and payment-card machines but not space-age scales or scanners (that's why tomatoes are simply 79 cents each whether they're big or small).

Butchers and bakers can't fit in the tent, so they're prepackaging meat and bread. And even though circled by a lockable chain-link fence, the store isn't selling alcohol or tobacco so not to tempt thieves.

The tent may seem a mere novelty amid historic destruction, but local leaders consider it important enough to list on their municipal website alongside links to police and fire department phone numbers, road and bridge closures and the Federal Emergency Management Agency.

Nearby Weston resident Roger Hochstin endured four days without electricity, then bailed out a flooded basement before driving this week to the Ludlow market.

"Under the circumstances, I think they did a great job" Hochstin said as he pushed a brimming shopping cart. "It's fully staffed and almost fully stocked."

The store is working out the kinks. Young staffers raised on barcodes and laser beams are learning how to stick price tags on individual items, then push register buttons to – ka-ching! – calculate a total.

("Shaw's Country Store," receipts say.)

"As the days go by," adds Williams, a grocer for 32 years, "we'll constantly assess what else we need."

Employees scanned one set of dark shelves, for example, only to find something missing.

It was literally a light-bulb moment.

NOTES FROM THE CAVENDISH CHASM
By Mary McCallum

(McCallum's piece aired on Vermont Public Radio on Oct. 11, 2011)

In Cavendish, I am one of the lucky ones. When Tropical Storm Irene swept across Vermont on August 28, I lost power and read by candle and lamplight as the wind lashed the forest of tall red pines around my house. I watched through rain splattered windows as scores of them swelled in waves, bending as one. Miraculously, none broke. My home was spared but the three roads and a bridge leading to it were not. Transformed into raging brown torrents, they washed away and left those of us in this backwoods neighborhood unable to drive out. But being inconvenienced couldn't compare with what many residents of my town endured.

The National Guard moved in for a month to rebuild destroyed roads and bridges, while the elementary school became a shelter that dished up three meals a day and served as Central Command for donated food, hastily formed work crews, flood updates and a community of shoulders to cry on. Although I was cut off for more than a week, I have a bicycle and I love to walk. The half mile trek to the washed out bridge and pedal into town became the new normal. Helping serve meals to work crews and displaced families made me feel connected to the history making event, and even a little useful.

As in scores of communities around Vermont, Irene generated local stories to be passed on for generations. I carry two iconic memories of the storm that are flecked with hope, humor and irony.

There is the moment when the owner of our bakery cafe, whose car was nearly filled with water, opened the door to let gallons of filthy flood water pour out. He got in and sat in the dripping driver's seat to ponder the magnitude of damage to the car, his parking

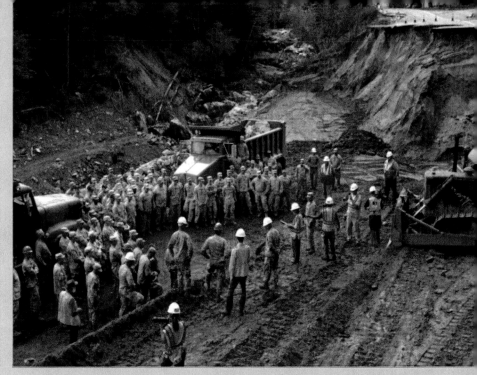

The Cavendish Chasm was one of many places exemplified by Irene – a small brook caused major damage, cutting off a crucial road.

Local contractors and the National Guard came together to repair the Cavendish Chasm and the road was in operation again within 10 weeks of Irene.

lot and his business. There, staring back at him at eye level sat a tiny survivor, also taking stock of its situation - a displaced mouse clung wearily to the top curve of the steering wheel. While mice aren't long distance swimmers, I imagined this tired refugee doing laps in the flooded car until help arrived.

The family next to the bakery suffered terrible damage to their basement and land. Over the years they had transformed their back acreage into a green oasis of winding paths, secret dells and hidden shady bowers with benches, sculpture, sparkly lights and flowers. You could get lost back there. Irene swept it all away, leaving behind a desert of sand, river stone, debris and mangled trees.

Days later, a crew of volunteers began the backbreaking labor of clearing it out and restoring the soil. They hauled stones and tree trunks, raked debris, planted grass and spread hay.

A worker looked up and noticed something orange snagged in a treetop. It was a book. Someone got it down and all stared in surprise at the title of the soggy volume. It was The Force of Nature. An ironic calling card left behind by Irene, who - it seems - just had to have the last word.

I carry two iconic memories of the storm that are flecked with hope, humor and irony.

November, and had spent much of the intervening months moving town documents and historical records there, culminating with a town party and celebration on August 27.

At the height of the storm the Millbrook building, which housed the historical society and a second-story apartment, was swept off its foundation and into the river, causing a blockage at the bridge that could have taken out the bridge as well as the lower half of the village. Thomas Fuller, Jr., who was out with a crew fortifying nearby riverbanks, quickly realized that the Millbrook House couldn't be saved. There was no way to bring it out of the water. With a heavy heart, Fuller used his excavator to smash it, sending it down river, along with personal items that had belonged to Silas Griffith, Vermont's first millionaire, old diaries, photographs, postcards and Pearl Buck's desk, gone to save a town and nearby Mount Tabor.

Bob Butler had a close call just two days later when he and Kenneth Clark, both also of Danby, were repairing a section of storm-damaged Route 7 in Clarendon. A flash flood swelled the Cold River and left them stranded on an island in the river, requiring an air rescue from the New York State Police helicopter

team. The men were part of a team working on Route 7 after floodwaters from Tropical Storm Irene engorged the Cold River where it runs underneath Vermont's major north-south route, causing a 30-foot deep chasm

Bob Butler and Kenneth Clark were rescued by helicopter from a flash flood a few days after Irene.

Rescuers evacuate a resident on State Street in Rutland.

in Route 7. While hundreds of calls were swamping the State Police dispatch center on McKinley Avenue in Rutland Town, the police barracks itself became a casualty of the storm. Dispatchers and troopers had to evacuate their headquarters as Otter Creek spilled over its banks. State Police moved into the Rutland City Police Department in the city's downtown and spent the day coordinating countywide crises while the city police oversaw evacuations in low-lying neighborhoods of the city. Above McKinley Avenue, the water had flooded Route 7, filling fields all around the Williams family farm.

Many Rutland neighborhoods were cut off as both the East and Otter Creeks crested and overflowed, flooding homes on Clover and Earl Street, as well as parts of Baxter, West, Meadow, State and School streets. With flooding on Route 7 north and south, Crescent, State and West streets out, and most of the city's bridges under water, there was no way in or out of Rutland. A garden on Earl Street that only hours before had neat rows of tomato and pepper plants was covered in a slime of mud; basements filled with the same noxious glop. Meadow Street Park was a sea of mud; resident Louis Ross escaped but had to move out and lost the tools and

equipment he needed for his painting business. Above the city, the Alpine Pipeline, which brings wastewater from Killington for treatment at the city's sewage plant, had been dismantled by floodwaters, threatening the city's water supply. For several days after the storm, Rutland residents were urged to conserve water.

Then, more tragedy. A father and son, Michael J. Garofano, 55, and Michael G. Garofano, 24, both of Rutland, drowned while checking intake valves at the Rutland water reservoir early Sunday afternoon. The

---

WAITING IN RUTLAND
Published in the Rutland Herald and Times Argus on Sept. 2, 2011
By BRENT CURTIS

Traci Beaudry thought she was ready for Irene after she bought canned goods and batteries.

But four days after the storm departed, her six-member family is living out of a motel room because her home on Meadow Street in Rutland is too toxic to return to.

"I knew it would be bad, but I didn't think it would be this bad," Beaudry said during a visit to her apartment Wednesday morning.

While images of collapsed homes have been broadcast nationwide, residents on low-lying streets in Rutland have been quietly digging out from floods that devastated whole neighborhoods.

The conditions on Meadow Street may be the worst in the city. While every other city street was reopened to traffic Wednesday, barriers still blocked the north half of Meadow Street where the sound of sump pumps droned and the stink of fuel oil from overturned tanks filled the air.

"It's too toxic to stay here," Louis Ross said, standing on the porch of his home overlooking the mud-covered fields of Meadow Street Park.

On Sunday and Monday, flood waters laden with mud, oil and raw sewage surged into the basement and first floor of a home that he recently paid a substantial sum to improve.

He has flood insurance, but the tools and equipment for his drywall and painting business were ruined, he said, and like Beaudry, he's living out of a motel room.

"We got hit the worst," said Ross, whose wife, children and stepfather have all been forced out of the home as well.

Just four doors down, Rosemary LaRose was in similar straights, but the elderly woman said she wasn't going anywhere.

"I spent one night out of my apartment and that was enough," she said, referring to her decision to evacuate Sunday night.

She returned Monday to find her first floor apartment untouched by the flood. But the water in the basement was almost up to the floorboards and a leaking oil tank that turned over in the basement filled her living quarters with fumes.

Her landlord advised her to leave. But LaRose said she and three of the other five tenants in the building had decided to ride it out.

"There's a lot of people suffering more in other parts of the state," she said.

That was a sentiment heard more than once this week from Rutland residents affected by the flood.

"I've heard it's a lot worse for other people whose houses are gone. At least I'm alive and have a home to go to," Water Street resident Mike Steele said.

Steele and all of his neighbors spent the day pumping water from their basements and scraping mud out of their driveways while waiting and hoping that electricians would give them the green light to turn their power back on.

Steele and his neighbors were sharing beers after a long day of what they described as a community cleanup.

"Everyone is pitching in, and the city came through earlier and scraped what they could out of people's driveways," said Water Street resident Steve Cushman.

On Meadow Street, Hearts and Minds Daycare owner Rebecca Wetmore praised residents on the street who helped her on Monday.

"The neighbors have been awesome down here," she said. "Everyone is helping each other out. That's pretty awesome when you think about what everyone is dealing with."

(top) The Rutland State Police emergency command center was flooded; (right) Residents of Clover Street in Rutland evacuate with what possessions they can carry, and (above) Cleveland Avenue in Rutland was underwater.

elder Garofano had grown up in Rutland and had been employed with the Rutland Department of Public Works since 1981. Described as exceptionally dedicated to his family and his job as the Rutland Water Treatment Plant supervisor, Garofano had apparently gone to the Mendon reservoir to make sure dirty water wasn't contaminating the city's water supply. His son accompanied him, not just because of the gravity of the situation but also because the two were quite close. It's believed the two men were swept away when a bank gave way along the Mendon Brook, which had swelled from its normal width of 16 feet to 10 times as wide. The elder Garofano's body was recovered the next day, but the body of the younger Garofano wasn't found until three weeks after the storm.

A THANK YOU MESSAGE FROM THE GAROFANO FAMILY
Written By Frank Urso

(Urso is brother-in-law to Michael J. Garofano and uncle to Michael G. Garofano, both of Rutland, who died while checking on Rutland City's water supplies for the Rutland Department of Public Works. This is the message delivered at their funeral Mass, Sept. 9, 2011)

From the Garofano Family
To the People of Rutland
And the people who came to help,
And to everyone in this church

Thank you so much.

So many have come to our aid, too numerous to mention in one day. But we know who you are.

Whether you work at Rutland City Hall
Or the Department of Public Works
Or the Fire Department
Or the Police Department
Or the Vermont State Police

Whether you are a member of the National Guard
Or the Colchester Search and Rescue Team
Or the New England K-9 Unit

Whether you work for Casella's or Markowski Excavating, Fabian Excavating
Or FEMA

Whether you helped in our search
Whether you provided us with food
Or hugs
Or simply shared our grief from a distance,

We are deeply grateful.

The Garofano family does not want to eulogize Michael Joseph Garofano
A simple man who was grounded like a rock in the love of his family and his sense of duty.

Nor does the family want to eulogize his son, Michael Gregory Garofano,
A beautiful young man, age 24, who was about to blossom like a flower in his mother's garden

No additional words are needed to brand their memories in our hearts and minds.

Instead, our Family wants all of you to resume your lives to the fullest,
Starting on this beautiful sunny day
And, thereafter, rain or shine, having been reminded how precious each day of our lives is and how precious our families and loved ones are,
And how precious our friends and neighbors are.

Rutland City Police officers honor the Garofanos.

North along Route 7, another tributary of the Otter Creek was rising in Brandon. Both the Watershed Tavern, formerly the well-known LaDuke's, and the Brandon House of Pizza were literally built over the river. By 5 p.m. Sunday, the river had moved the House of Pizza more than 20 feet from its foundation where it came to rest halfway in the road and against Ricky Rowe's barbershop and water was literally flowing in the tavern's back door and out the front. Rowe, 82, who lives upstairs and has operated the business for 55 years, refused to leave as the waters rose around the old barbershop but left it standing. Videos of this disaster were downloaded to the Internet within a few minutes. In short time, also, floodwaters had destroyed two parks that had represented the town's recent revitalization and undermined the Briggs Carriage Building.

Route 4 is one of the few east-west roads in southern Vermont and there's a reason for that – building it was a challenge, given the topography of the region. Rebuilding huge swaths of it would prove challenging in the days after Irene. While Route 4 had some washouts between the New York border and Rutland, these were temporary inconveniences in comparison to the devastation to the highway and towns along Route 4 from Mendon to Quechee. A major wash out at the crest of the highway past Sugar and Spice was the first of dozens of giant obstacles.

The washout not only took a huge chunk out of Route 4 near the Mendon Town Office but floodwaters carried six acres of land from a home owned by Todd Keehan and his wife Josiane Deletine, making their once private property an island. In the days that followed, not only were they stranded but they also faced a problem that would be repeated over and over throughout storm-damaged towns, for those who had lost homes and even those who had not – what was the value of lost land, of scenic resources, of privacy? And in the coming weeks and months, difficult questions would need to be addressed as property owners sought reduced assessments and property tax abatements. For some, it was total loss – no home and no property or not enough to build upon. And for people like Keehan and Deletine, who had purchased their home not for the house itself but for its beautiful park-like property, there was the question of whether to stay or go, and if the answer was to leave, what value did the now storm-scoured property have for resale?

MENDON COUPLE MOURNS LOST WAY OF LIFE
Published in the Rutland Herald and Times Argus
on Sept. 15, 2011
By YVONNE DALEY

It's the raspberries that Todd Keehan laments. His wife, Josiane Deletine, cries for the daylilies and daisies that once lined their road.

They say there is no monetary value they can place on those raspberries, the gardens, the weeping willow trees, tall pines and lilacs, all gone along with the couple's privacy when Mendon Brook turned from a gentle mountain stream to a ravaging river in a matter of hours during Tropical Storm Irene.

The brook jumped its banks, rerouted itself, took out the bridge to their home and a roughly six-acre field that, with its trees and gardens spreading on either side of the brook, resembled a parkland and provided seclusion from busy Route 4.

Keehan and Deletine know they are lucky. Stone retaining walls built by previous owners and expanded during the seven years they have lived there saved the house, now quite visible from the highway.

The couple met in Westport, CT., and after a decade together decided to move to Vermont in 2007. They visited many properties, always looking for one that combined access to the woods and mountains, to skiing and hiking, with a farmhouse and the opportunity to raise vegetables and have a few chickens.

When they saw the Mendon property on July 4, they "knew as soon as we parked at the bridge. I said, this is it," Deletine recalls in her French accent. She's originally from a small town near Paris.

But, although the couple love their house, they didn't buy it for the house, but rather for the property, land that is now a boulder and rubble-filled mess that they fear may be polluted and may not grow grass and trees for a long time. A FEMA official said they are only eligible for $600 to repair a damaged retaining wall.

Cy Dailey, district advisor for property valuation at the Vermont Department of Taxes, says "everyone's been talking about this question, from coffeeshops to Montpelier," the question being what do people do who have lost value to their property but not their house or other structures.

Individuals like Keehan and Deletine can ask their town officials to reassess their property, a move Dailey predicts many homeowners in Vermont will choose in the next few months as many have lost land or have spoiled land due to the flooding. Property reassessments can, in turn, negatively affect town revenues, just when towns need more money to respond to Irene's damage, he said.

Mendon Town Administrator Sara Tully said two structures in town had substantial damage; beyond that, many had minor damage from flooded basements and some have property damage. The town has had no requests for reassessment but she expects some in the future, which in turn could affect the tax base.

"As those properties get reassessed downward, the amount of taxes to be collected over the next couple of years will stay the same or increase to respond to the storm," Tully said. "We expect to get some of it back from FEMA and we are working diligently to assess our expenses. We were declared a disaster so FEMA will pay a percentage of our expenses," which include 19 road projects, not including Route 4, which is the responsibility of the Vermont Agency of Transportation.

Keehan and Delatine weren't the only ones who cried over the damaged property. Kris Hubenet grew up in that house in Mendon; indeed, if you mention the property to local residents, they usually identify it as Dr. Hubenet's house after Dr. Bernard Hubenet who bought the house in 1949.

Kris Hubenet likes to tell the story of how her parents chose the house – again, as much for the property's natural resources as the house itself. Bernard Hubenet and his wife Frances were looking for a home in the area when he decided to start his orthopedic practice here. One day he and a companion went trout fishing in a pool above the Mendon house. They caught their limit that day, and the next, then saw the for-sale sign.

Fortunately, Frances Hubenet liked the house and property too. To safeguard the house, Bernard Hubenet added on to existing retaining walls, walls that may date back to when the property was part of the estate of Edward Hastings Ripley, the general in command of the Union occupation of Richmond during the Civil War.

It was Bernard Hubenet who dug up willow seedlings from Whipple Hollow Road in West Rutland and hemlocks from along Route 4, planting them along the riverbank as a screen against the highway, the trees that Keehan watch "fall like dominoes, one after another."

Kris Hubenet recalls that Mendon Brook jumped its banks in June 1973 when she was a freshman at the University of Missoula and her father was visiting her and fishing. Her mother moved a car to the other side of the bridge onto Route 4 before the bridge went out.

"That wouldn't have helped us any," Keehan said, as dump trucks, dwarfed by the magnitude of the devastation, moved the piles of rubble and broken asphalt that once was Route 4 around. "I'd give up the cars in a heartbeat to have those berry bushes back, to have what we once thought was ours. It would take a lifetime to restore that."

River Road in Killington was buckled and broken by flood waters.

But questions like those, while important to homeowners and towns alike, were put off while more essential issues were addressed. The 41-mile-long Ottauquechee River rises in the Green Mountains in the town of Killington and flows eastwardly toward Windsor County, passing through Bridgewater, Woodstock and Quechee, eventually flowing into the Connecticut River at Hartland. As it filled with torrents of water rushing down the mountainsides, it left a path of destruction that seemed like a scene from an apocalyptic movie rather than the results of a one-day storm. Throughout Killington, the largest ski area in the east, more than 300 guests and another 100 employees were stranded in hotels and condominiums as thousand-foot sections of Route 4 were smashed, blocking passage either east or west. The K-1 Lodge's Superstar Pub had structural damage when the Roaring Brook breached its banks, dislodging a portion of the building. Up on the Access Road to the Killington Ski Area and down along side streets, town roads were turned into corrugated chunks of mangled pavement.

Property surrounding a small house along Route 4 across from River Road was quickly eaten up by the river and then the house went floating underneath a bridge that leads into the section of town where the Killington town office and library are located. Out-of-state residents had just signed a contract to purchase it. The house and other debris that had been dragged down the mountain by the renegade river clogged the bridge and sent water sluicing to either side. Within an hour, Route 4 had turned into what one resident described as "a veritable class-5 rapids" that tore away the asphalt and left a tangle of mud, trees and debris. Muck-encased boulders hugged the Kokopelli Inn just down the road where once pretty gardens and lawn had been. Along River Road, many houses and yards were badly flooded.

Governor Shumlin speaks to volunteers before they head out to help flood victims in Waterbury.

CHOIR OF ANGELS

Ann Wallen, an 89-year-old artist, had lived on Route 4 near River Road in Killington for 50 years. Her home was built in the 1830s as the toll house; the barn alongside was the blacksmith shop where travelers changed horses before making the trip over the mountain into Rutland. During the day of the storm, Wallen dug a trench along the side of the house as she had done in the 1973 flood to keep the river from washing out the walkway to her kitchen and made note that she was low in candles. Concerned that the Ottauquechee River might flood, she decided not to put her car in its usual spot in the barn but instead parked it on high ground as she had also done in '73.

As the rain fell, she could hear rocks crashing in the river. It sounded like thunder, but every time she checked, that ditch she'd made seemed to be working fine. When it got dark, she lit the five Christmas candles she'd found and sat in the kitchen reading with the storm ravaging all around, feeling quite safe and snug. She never heard the house across the road go out, swept away in the roiling water. So, of course, she didn't realize that house's demise had saved her and her house by clogging the bridge at River Road, sending the Ottauquechee into two directions. One branch coursed down River Road where it did its damage; the other tore a chasm in Route 4 and left a field of debris and broken trees miles downstream.

Around 10, she checked the trench again, then went to bed. She slept quite soundly. She didn't hear the tree come down, shattering her car.

I've often said I have a guardian angel. That day I must have had a whole choir of angels watching out for me.

Early the next morning, she thought she heard someone calling her name and went outside to look. There was her friend and neighbor, Duane Finger. He'd risked his own safety to rescue her, jumping over the river and navigating across chunks of asphalt to her house. Finger brought Wallen back to the house off the Killington Access Road where he lives with his wife Jill Dye.

"It was like the Perils of Pauline, us hopping over the broken concrete together," Wallen recalls, referring to the classic damsel in distress motion picture.

As it turned out, she didn't have a drop of water in her basement but couldn't get back home for four days. "If it had happened differently, I don't know where I'd be today or if I'd even be," she says. "I've often said I have a guardian angel. That day I must have had a whole choir of angels watching out for me. And then, Duane coming to rescue me. He and Jill were so wonderful, angels also."

Route 4 East from Killington into Bridgewater Flats was ripped apart.

RED THINGS
Oct. 10, 2011
Written By Mary T. Holland

(Holland is a lister in the town of Killington; her home is at the base of Pico Mountain. She was stranded for more than a week due to shattered roads, then had the job of checking on properties throughout the town.)

Seeing the sudden flash of red leaves among the increasingly bright golds and oranges lifts my spirit. I am thrilled by nature's ability to endure. The foliage, late and sparse, is magical in its normalcy.

We sent out the word that Vermont is "open for business." I don't want our visitors to be disappointed. Everyone had been working so hard to pull it all together.

The command center in Killington Town offices.

I didn't want the foliage to be one more loss due to Irene. I feel the brightening of colors as a benediction.

It is a curious, heartbreaking journey living through the hurricane. I support my fellow survivors by listening to their stories, by bearing witness to their pain and acknowledging their heroism. We are all heroic in our survival of the storm's traumatic aftermath. We are kinder. We look out for one another.

There is pride in our ability to do for ourselves until help arrives. The sense of community is strengthened by the need to organize, to do something. That helps calm the frantic energy following the news that we are stranded, an island in the middle of the land locked state of Vermont.

During the days and weeks that follow we all struggle with the reality of limited resources and an uncertain future. So the decision that we would be ready to invite the world to come see "our" Vermont was ballsy and optimistic not unlike most of choices for moving here in the first place.

Appropriate that as this Columbus Day is celebrated for the discovery of our new world it is also celebrating the rediscovery how precious this place and this way of life is to me.

We are stranded, an island in the middle of the land locked state of Vermont.

Further along Route 4 in West Bridgewater, the Long Trail Brewery was flooded as was the 180-year-old Bridgewater Mill. Both buildings had water in their basements and extensive debris in their parking lots but no structural damage. The damage to the Irving gas station in Bridgewater, however, was almost incomprehensible. The station's parking lot looked like it had melted then solidified into chunks of asphalt while the building itself was a-kilter. To either side of the river, homes were demolished and lawns and gardens had been replaced by expansive stretches of disgusting runoff, mounds of debris, the refuse from dismantled homes upstream. A flood-damaged section of Route 100 also cut West Bridgewater off from Ludlow.

Woodstock's downtown south of Bridgewater Corners fared fairly well although there was extensive flooding in basements, but four iconic businesses on the western side of town – the Woodstock Farmer's Market, the Vermont Standard, Dead River Company and the White Cottage – looked as if the river had not only gone through them but in doing so rearranged their interiors, taking with it 200 propane tanks, some weighing a couple of thousand pounds, refrigerators and picnic tables, stoves and a grease filtration system, tens of thousands of dollars' worth of groceries.

WOODSTOCK BUSINESSES WORKING TO RECOVER

Published in the Rutland Herald and Times Argus on Oct. 14, 2011
By YVONNE DALEY

In about a month, the Woodstock Farmers' Market has raised about $250,000 to help rebuild the store, using an ingenious offer similar to Community Supported Agriculture memberships that have buoyed local farmers for the past decade or more.

Supporters of the market, badly damaged in Tropical Storm Irene, can purchase Irene Cards valued at $25 to $5,000. Once the market reopens, customers who buy a card worth up to $1,000 will get a 10 percent discount on purchases, while those who pay more than $1,000 will get a 15 percent discount. The cards are good for three years.

"It's a pretty good return on your money," owner Patrick Crowl said last week in an interview in the market's temporary quarters near Woodstock's downtown where he described a harrowing experience of rescuing computers as the raging Ottauquechee River flooded his business and that of three other long-established businesses along Route 4 just west of the village – the Dead River Company, the Vermont Standard and the White Cottage Snack Bar.

IRVING

IRVING

3.75⁹ clean regular

4.09⁹ clean diesel

Bridgewater gas station.

Crowl and John Hurley, owner of the White Cottage, as well as Dead River, a propane company headquartered in Portland, ME., plan to rebuild. Phil Camp, publisher of The Standard, Vermont's oldest weekly newspaper, has determined his building is a total loss.

Camp moved his operation to office space in Westerdale, a section of Woodstock, where a determined staff of eight along with stringers from neighboring towns managed to do what the paper has since 1853 – meet a weekly deadline. The Standard published a 52-page paper full of stories, informal reports from outlying towns and dozens of photographs the Friday after the storm, less than 24 hours after they got back their internet service.

Dead River Company

Michael Schmell, district manager of Dead River, said the storm destroyed about 5,000 square feet of the propane company's original building, which is being rebuilt. The power of the river astounded him as turbulent water yanked a six-foot, chainlink fence from its cement foundation, then hurled as many as 200 tanks, some weighing a couple of thousand pounds, downriver.

Most have been found, but some tanks made their way as far as Bellows Falls. Schmell said it was just a rumor that one tank had traveled as far as Long Island Sound. The sound people heard was not tanks exploding but rather releasing propane, which vaporizes in air.

While he said there was no legal prohibition against storing propane tanks in its Woodstock location post-Irene, Dead River is looking for another storage facility.

White Cottage Snack Bar

Hurley has a bigger obstacle ahead of him, given that the floodwaters went through his building, causing such serious structural damage he fears he might need to rebuild. Hurley lives in Killington and had quite a time getting to his business on Monday morning after Irene.

He found huge trees inside the building along with several feet of mud, walls pushed out and almost everything inside and out – 17 picnic tables, soda and ice cream machines, stoves and a grease filtration system – simply gone. Even the stand's sign had disappeared.

For Hurley, who bought the White Cottage in a partnership 23 years ago, owned it for 12 years with his partner, then sold it, then bought it back about 10 years ago, the White Cottage has long been a labor of love, but he will need his insurance company to come through if he is to reopen by next summer.

"I can't say enough good about the state," he said, explaining that he received a loan from the Small Business Administration within five days of applying while he's still awaiting to hear from his insurance provider.

Still, he's determined to rebuild as soon as possible. To that end, he will present his plans to the Woodstock Planning Commission later this month. "I want to start November 1," he said. "I don't want to wait till spring, miss the summer and lose my livelihood," not to mention that of his employees.

Woodstock Farmers' Market

Crowl was a ski instructor living in Colorado in 1992 when a Thanksgiving Eve fire destroyed the original structure his father, Jack Crowl, had established. When Jack Crowl told his son he thought the job of rebuilding and running the still-nascent business seemed too daunting, Patrick Crowl decided to move to Vermont and operate the market himself.

Now, 19 years later, the market grosses roughly $5 million a year and is an essential part of the community, selling not just organic fruit, vegetables, grain, meat and seafood, but also organic wines, sandwiches and baked goods, and plants.

After Croll heard that the Ottauquechee had breached Route 4, it took him three tries along three different routes before he and his wife Stacy Bebo could get to the market, traveling with their 10-month-old son Liam.

When he arrived, he found his mother Dana Crowl in the parking lot snapping photos. "Mom," he remembers saying, "get out of here." She left with Liam as Bebo and Crowl set about rescuing their computer and back-up systems.

Meanwhile, friends were trying to get items off the ground. "I realized we were past that point when I looked out the window and the river was at window height. We threw the breakers and got out of there. I felt like the captain of a ship that was going down," Crowl recalls.

Within minutes, a large ice machine and storage sheds floated away and were gone. Meanwhile, propane tanks from Dead River were spinning and hissing with whitegas coming out of them.

Crowl had one thought – to get his family home to safety. That, however, was impossible because of closed roads. It took another day before they got home.

Fortunately, his buildings can be repaired and he had flood insurance. Still, the market lost roughly $1 million in contents while it had about $350,000 in outstanding bills. The market employs 45 people.

"People have been wonderful, calling and writing and stopping by," Crowl said. "The Irene Card is a way to say thank you while helping us rebuild and restock so we can be back in business as soon as possible."

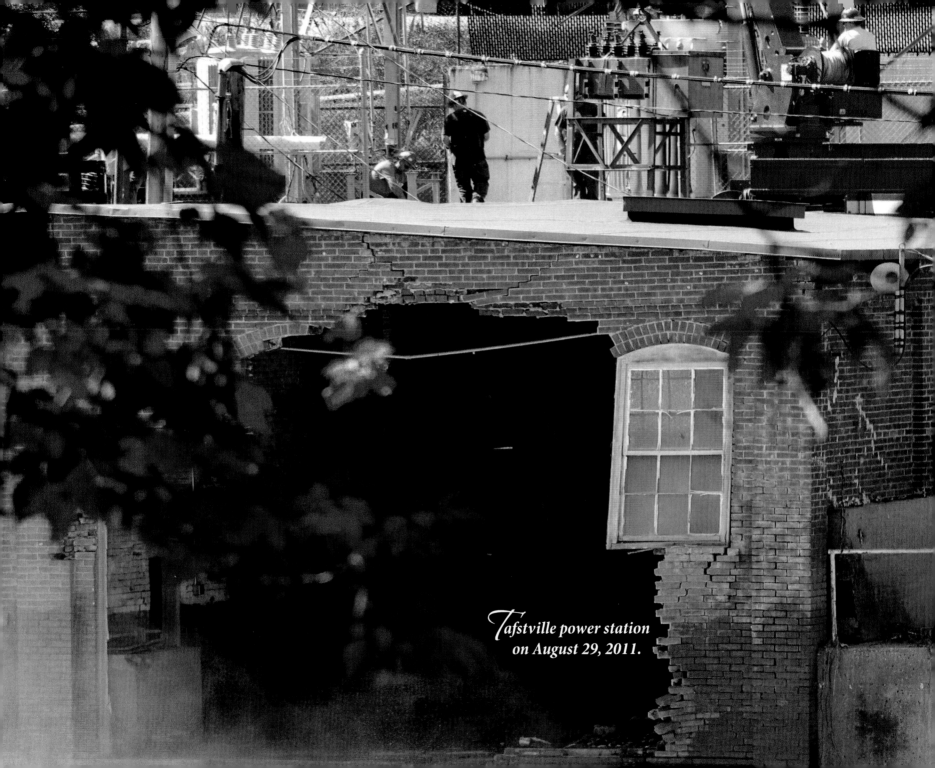

Tafstville power station on August 29, 2011.

WOODSTOCK MOVING AHEAD
Published in the Rutland Herald and Times Argus on Oct. 14, 2011
By YVONNE DALEY

Woodstock Town Planner Michael Brands is still amazed at the damage Tropical Storm Irene caused and the speed with which the town has recovered, especially as Woodstock businesses depend so much on tourist dollars during foliage season.

At one point, half the town roads were damaged, many impassible, with as much as half-mile washouts. About 58 homes received major damage, including 20 of 39 mobile homes in Riverside Park, located along the Ottauquechee River.

Along with the closing of the Taftsville covered bridge until it can be rebuilt in 2014, several other bridges in town were badly damaged, but now all roads are open to traffic, some at reduced speed while repairs continue. Brands expects the town will receive FEMA funds to offset some of the cost of rebuilding roads.

Meanwhile, Courtney Lowe, director of sales and marketing at the Woodstock Inn, described the extensive work being done to repair damage on what's referred to as the garden level of the inn, its grounds and especially its golf course.

The Woodstock Inn was closed for five weeks after Irene, but is now open on all floors, except the garden level; the golf course will remain closed for the season.

Lowe's home overlooks the golf course; he watched as the normally pacific Kedron Brook overflowed, turning parts of the golf course into a sea of silt, damaging cart bridges and essentially destroying all 51 sand traps.

Inside the inn, water flooded conference rooms and 13 guest rooms on the garden level, all of which have been emptied of furnishings and stripped down to the rafters for restoration. Fortunately, the lobby, the remaining 129 guestrooms and the restaurant were untouched.

Lowe explained that the inn could have been open much sooner but its electric mains, located in the area that was flooded, had to be custom-made in El Paso, Texas, shipped, installed, and then inspected.

"From a p.r. standpoint, it was interesting to get people to see that the town of Woodstock was open for business while also saying that we are responding to the flood," Lowe explained. He said the inn's best tool was Facebook where its page had about 500 followers prior to Irene and 4000 during and after the storm.

"We kept posting updates. You've got to be real," in situations like this, he said. "The support from not just local people and businesses, but guests that have been here, was just so heartwarming."

Online readers both within and outside Woodstock also kept track of the flood and recovery at Woodstock Early Bird, a website Woodstock resident Julia Carlisle started in June to fill a hole she saw in news coverage of local government.

For years, Carlisle has been dividing her time between Vermont, where she has worked as a ski reporter, and Juno, Alaska, where she has worked as a park ranger and hiking guide at Glacier Bay National Park and as an NPR correspondent after a career as a radio producer for ABC news in New York.

Since June, she's been building up subscribers to her free blog at http://woodstockearlyworm.wordpress.com/ where she posts stories and photos about planning commission and school board meetings, obituaries, news of accidents, town unemployment statistics and feature stories on local events and people.

Until Tropical Storm Irene, she had 50 subscribers and dozens of hits a day. The day after the flood, she had thousands of hits in one day. While the pace has slowed down, the site now has 385 subscribers and may get as many as a thousand hits in a day.

Route 4 in Woodstock by the Farmer's Market.

The White Cottage in Woodstock.

GONE IN 15 MINUTES
Published in the Rutland Herald and Times Argus on Sep. 3, 2011
By CRISTINA KUMKA

Suzy Krawczyk woke up on her West Woodstock farm Monday morning to find 200 of her chickens buried alive in the mud. Lauren Spresser ran from her mobile home with her three cats, a ferret and a dog, moments before it was swallowed by the rising Ottauquechee River.

And Sigurd Swanson, born and raised in Woodstock, drove from Walpole, N.H., Thursday to see what happened to the tame river he knew as a child.

"We used to raft down that river and I've never seen it that like before," Swanson said, staring at the remains of the office of the Vermont Standard, owned by his friend Phil Camp.

The office's front wall was peeled away from the rest of the building like a sardine can.

On Thursday, the water was calm in the river that runs along Bridgewater into Woodstock, running over the wheels of an overturned car that lay bottom up on the riverbed, the black rubber glistening in the sunlight.

Disaster didn't discriminate in Woodstock.

From the wealthy to the middle class to the poor, Tropical Storm Irene affected the community in its entirety and has made people here closer friends.

Krawcyk, a mother of five and owner of the Thymeless Herbs Farm, said although many of her animals have died, many of her pigs, roosters, hens and cats and dogs have been placed in foster situations until she can decontaminate the land off of which they eat.

She doesn't know when that will happen. She doesn't have flood insurance. The company representative told her she didn't need it.

When her father helped her renovate her farmhouse years back, they called the project "Beautify Route 4."

Krawcyk cried when she said "beautify."

The town of Woodstock had no running water Thursday. Some of the historic homes on River Street, Maple Street, Elm Street were flooded, along with the Woodstock Inn and Resort at the center of town.

The inn is closed until further notice and the humming of pumps moving water out of the inn's ground-floor conference rooms was all that could be heard on the street.

The back porches of homes in the most affluent section of town were hanging into the river or floating down it.

Picturesque, vibrant green waterfront properties were turned into matte brown beaches.

The flat rock behind The White Cottage, loved by many townspeople for generations, was washed away. The town pool looked more like a muddy lake.

Outside of downtown, homes in the Riverside Mobile Home Park were washed away from their cement beds.

Woodstock Farmer's Market cleanup.

All that's left of Debbie Urbino's home is muddy shoe prints on her rug and in her hallways.

She pointed at a dirt mound that used to be her lush flower garden and a deck that was the envy of the park.

The water pushed her car into her mobile home, denting the rear end.

It's all gone now.

"It's hard when you've worked so hard for everything you have and it's gone in 15 minutes," Urbino said.

Back downtown, Gordon Pine, a Woodstock resident who volunteered all day, said not all was lost. The Middle Bridge, a covered bridge by the town green, remained and so did the community's spirit.
"It's the New England way. People mind their own business and they might not know your name but they will help you when you need it," Pine said.

At a community supper on the town green at 4 p.m. Thursday, two camouflaged military trucks passed by, one carrying cases of bottled water.

The crowd, plates of heaping food in their hands, looked up almost in unison and cheered.

The soldier driving the water truck honked his horn, then after perhaps 10 seconds of celebration, he and the crowd got back to business.

Three of the building owners surveyed their properties in the following days and decided to try to rebuild but the Vermont Standard, Vermont's oldest weekly newspaper, would move to another location.

Further downstream, the village of Quechee was flooded badly by the normally placid Ottauquechee River, so long its calling card. The river's torrent was full-bore by the time it reached there, not only damaging the town's covered bridge and nearby buildings but sewer and water lines as well. The Quechee Club building was one of the few structures in the small downtown to be spared. Destruction was especially extensive at the Simon Pearce restaurant and glassblowing facility, whose dramatic location overlooking the river and the fact that some of the operation were located at the lower level of the mill contributed to its partial demise. The glassblowing facility, hydro turbine, and some of the kitchen operations had significant damage, but the mill, and the facility's restaurant and retail store were relatively spared.

Quechee is a village in Hartford; damage in Quechee contributed to Hartford's overall property loss of almost $5 million.

Other towns along Route 100 had similar versions of the devastation.

In Pittsfield, population 423, Rachel Fredette and her boyfriend Sean Krevetski were watching the rain swell the river behind their apartment. Their power went out and they went outside and saw their neighbor's house being undercut. He had taken his camper to higher ground, but left cars in the garage, which were in danger of being swept away. They tried to get in to remove the cars, but every door was locked, so another neighbor grabbed a chainsaw, cut two holes in the garage door, looped a chain through it and pulled the door off. He then pulled the cars to safety, Fredette said. Then the house fell in the river.

Pittsfield, a neighbor to Killington, was isolated, roads and bridges, including a privately owned covered bridge, gone; 10 homes were badly damaged or a total loss. In the first days, with few getting in and out of this town and devastation to its neighboring towns, little was known of the extent of the damage. Stockbridge too was in bad shape. Much of Route 107, which winds along the White River, was gone. At least 12 homes in Bethel — including several that survived the 1927 flood — were badly damaged or destroyed.

In Rochester, floodwaters not only wrecked Route 100 and took out the bridge to Route 73 but also unearthed about 50 coffins, sending some into the river where remains spilled into plain view. With several homes lost and dozens stranded, no power and no access to the outside world, this problem seemed like a cruel burden. Penny Parrish who owns the Skip Mart in Rochester, said, "It's like one of those movies, 'Armageddon.'"

Returning to their resting place in Rochester.

WORKERS ABLE TO REACH ROCHESTER
Published in the Rutland Herald and Times Argus
on Sept. 1, 2011
By GORDON DRITSCHILO AND
VYTO STARINSKAS

Jon Graham's house fell on him. "We'd already evacuated my daughters," said Graham, who, before Tropical Storm Irene, lived on Robinson Drive. "Our cats were still in there, so my wife and I went back in - finally found them, because they were hiding."

Graham said he was following his wife out, cat in hand, when he spotted the bag holding his laptops and most of his family's important papers.

"I stepped back to get it and the house just went," he said. "I was thrown into the back of the house, where there was water, but a bookcase kept the rubble from going on top of me."

Graham said he was pulled out the last few feet.

"It's an experience," he said. "Our house didn't flood. It fell into the river because the river cut the ground out from under it. We lost 10 feet of yard, easily. ... This house survived the '27 flood, all the floods we've had in the past 10 years - never a problem at all. This was a totally different animal."

In the initial days, the issue of what to do with the disinterred had to wait while several residents in need of kidney dialysis were airlifted out. In normal times, the town is fairly remote, nestled as it is between mountains along a branch of the White River on Route 100. Irene transformed that river, scenic in all seasons, into a churning machine that swiped homes downstream and took giant bites out of the asphalt. When the storm was over, property losses alone in this town amounted to nearly $5 million.

Rochester homeowner, Jon Graham, stands in front of his house describing his escape from floodwaters.

Rochester was beginning to connect with the outside world Wednesday. The town at the edge of the Green Mountain National Forest had been isolated for two days - though one resident described medical teams from Dartmouth-Hitchcock coming in by helicopter - when a crew of 25 workers from Central Vermont Public Service Corp. rolled in.

"We're going to get about 40 trucks in here today and start putting everything back together," CVPS spokesman Steve Costello said. "Virtually all the towns we were not able to get into we're into now."

Costello said the crew set out from Rutland and got to Rochester via Hancock.

Sandy Lincoln (center) with bakery employee Anna Labejsza (left), and customer Jeanie Levitan, who works at Inner Traditions Publishing Co., refuge from the storm.

"We went through a bunch of back roads," he said. "You couldn't come here from Ripton."

Costello said the substation in Rochester was destroyed, but a portable one was en route by tractor-trailer truck. While the utility had expected power to be out for weeks, Costello said Wednesday it should be back in days, though it was hard to offer estimates for individual customers due to the extent of the damage.

"We can't get everywhere, but where we can get, we have an army of people we can throw at it," he said.

Along Route 100, which was open Wednesday from Hancock into Rochester, some of the houses appeared destroyed. Others had been lifted from their foundations by the rising storm waters.

Spraypaint on a garage door near the destroyed substation read "keep out" and "don't remove anything."

The river broke away the edge of the town cemetery, washing up about 20 caskets and leaving some of them on the riverbed. Cemetery caretaker Sue Flewelling said some bodies were still missing.

Thirty people carrying plastic gas cans lined up outside a downtown gas station. People with food-filled shopping carts walked down Route 100. Residents constructed a makeshift bridge out of logs and lumber to connect Route 100 to Route 73.

VOICES OF IRENE
By Vyto Starinskas,
Staff Photographer

I can't sleep. I am waking up at 4:30 a.m. Once even at 3:30. I used to sleep like a baby and never woke up before 6. But the voices keep talking to me. The voices of people who just watched their homes destroyed by a raging river and have no flood insurance. The voices of people whose dreams and memories are covered in mud and are in need of healing. It's the 9/11 anniversary and 14 days after Tropical Storm Irene wrecked Vermont. So Vermont's tragedy was small compared to 9/11. But Friday I covered the funeral for Michael Garofano, the Department of Public Works' worker who was killed inspecting the flood waters with his son, also Michael. Tell me that it isn't as big as 9/11 for that family? So on a personal note: I have covered the flood 14 straight days. My living space is a mess. My clothes are all wrinkled in a pile and I have gotten doctor-confirmed poison ivy tromping through woods to isolated towns. But I keep hearing the voices. Like Jon Graham's or Brian Halligan's, who lost their entire homes in rushing floodwaters but, on the other hand, are lucky to be alive. I keep hearing all the "THANK YOUs." That is all I heard when I went to flood-torn Pittsfield, Rochester and Killington right after the flood. In the first few days, I was the only "clean" person in town. "Thank you for coming to see us," the voices would say. "Thank you for getting the word out," they would add. They were all covered in dirt and had smiles as wide as the Grand Canyon, despite the nearby homes tossed in the mud in Pittsfield, a home collapsed like a deck of cards in Rochester and a home devoured by a river in Killington. So last Saturday (Sept. 8), the town had a wedding at the firehouse in Pittsfield. Good for them. It must have been glorious. I had to cover a Mount St. Joseph football game. But that's OK. I can see the smiles on the townspeople's faces without actually being there. Watching Pittsfield residents work through the flood was amazing. They were organized. Respectful. Caring. Pittsfield held elementary school classes and had "haircut day" on their town green. Residents met helicopter food-drops. Pickup caravans were formed to deliver the emergency food shipments to stranded neighbors. I have been to Pittsfield town meetings and their town meeting lunches are the best. The baked beans get me back there every year. There will be a new electricity at every town meeting now. New friends among flatlanders and old-timers. People who saved each others' lives and then helped each other rebuild. A human bond that no one else will understand. Talk about turning a negative into a positive. "HERE COMES THE BRIDE..."

Vyto Starinskas, Rutland Herald photographer.

North along Route 100, John Kimmich, the co-owner with his wife of the Alchemist Pub & Brewery in Waterbury, had just poured himself a Holy Cow IPA Sunday night when he heard a banging from the pub's basement. When he opened the door he found kegs of beer bobbing in water that reached the top of the basement stairs. His heart sank. He finished his beer and locked the door on the way out. When he returned the next day, the pub was destroyed.

Moretown Town Clerk Cherilyn Lamson's home outside of town was unharmed; she didn't even know about the damage in the valley until the road foreman called the next morning and told her to put on her mud boots. When she arrived at the town office the next morning, watermarks showed that the Mad River had brought five and a half feet of water into the building; everything inside was ruined. In the months after the flood, town documents were freeze-dried in an effort to save as many as possible.

What Lamson surveyed outside was equally bad; almost no building in the downtown had been unharmed. The firehouse had been flooded; the schoolhouse was a wreck. The post office and the handsome century-old homes along the town's main streets had filled with floodwater and mud, contents in basements destroyed and, in many, possessions on the first floor also gone. Several parts of town were isolated because culverts had washed out.

The storm destroyed two bridges and 19 roads; the Moretown Mountain Road connecting Northfield and Montpelier was annihilated. Along Route 2 on the way to Waterbury, there was severe damage to houses and an auto repair shop. Snow Fire, a local Subaru dealer, lost most of its cars.

Sections of Montpelier were evacuated as the North Branch of the Winooski River overflowed its banks, but major damage was avoided. To the east, Green Mountain Power officials were keeping a close eye on the Marshfield Dam, which was in danger of overflowing, or, worst case, bursting. The dam ultimately held, but GMP's emergency contact list and procedures were not up to date, and many residents were evacuated.

Meanwhile, in Waterbury, the 19th-century brick campus housing the State Office Complex, where 1,200 state employees worked, and the Vermont State Hospital was a scene of disaster with oil-contaminated water filling the 500,000-square-foot facility's warren-like basement and mud coating the first floor in a slimy mess. The hospital had been evacuated during the storm, placing a burden on local hospitals throughout the state that took in individuals with mental health problems. Computer systems for the Department of Public Safety and the Agency of Natural Resources were removed from the saturated building while workers were sent to other locations to try to reconstruct not only their own records and processes but deal with the damage from Tropical Storm Irene.

As elsewhere, there was so much damage in Waterbury that local officials were overwhelmed. More than 100 buildings in the downtown alone had been flooded and a host of businesses between Route 2 and 100 were partially if not fully damaged. With property damage alone in Waterbury estimated at more than $9 million, uncertainties about whether the State Office Complex could or would be used again increased the town's financial concerns.

**WATERBURY TOWN SCRAMBLES
TO BOUNCE BACK**
**Published in the Rutland Herald and Times Argus
on Aug. 30, 2011**
By THATCHER MOATS

Waterbury and several towns in the Mad River Valley were inundated with floodwater Sunday, which knocked out bridges and electricity and left behind a slimy layer of mud on the streets and in homes and businesses. Waterbury Town Manager Bill Shepeluk said that within roughly two hours, Waterbury went from having no roads covered in water to having more than 4 feet of water on Elm Street and about 2 feet of water on Main Street.

"Things really started to go downhill at 6 o'clock," said Shepeluk.

With the water rising and Green Mountain Power worried it might have to release overflow water from the Marshfield dam, Waterbury officials evacuated numerous streets in the downtown area Sunday evening, including the Whalley Trailer Park near the intersection of Route 100 and North Main Street.

Roughly 100 people flocked to a shelter at Thatcher Brook Primary School, where many of them spent the night on gymnastics mats in the school gym.

Shepeluk said that in his 23 years as town manager in Waterbury, he's never seen anything like the flooding he witnessed this week.

"No, absolutely not," he said. "I've talked to several people and they say it hasn't been this bad since 1927."

The basement and first floor of the Waterbury town offices were flooded and reeked of fuel oil today, as did parts of Main Street.

With the town offices uninhabitable, municipal officials were hauling computer equipment into Thatcher Brook Primary School to establish a makeshift office.

The town's pump station, which is next to the Thatcher Brook and pumps wastewater to the wastewater treatment plant, was knocked out by floodwaters, said Shepeluk. He was asking residents to conserve water as a result.

Flooding also knocked out the Green Mountain Power substation, and the town was still without electricity today.

The town's new fire station on Main Street was flooded but suffered no apparent damage, said Shepeluk.

The main damage to town infrastructure was the pump station and the municipal offices, said Shepeluk. No bridges were washed out, and roads were not badly damaged, he said.

Shepeluk had heard no reports of injury.

The town reopened Main Street at about 8:30 a.m. today.

Waterbury resident Andy Fuller, a 59-year-old who lives at 16 Main St., missed much of the drama.

"I slept through it and didn't even know it was in my backyard until I woke up and it was a swimming pool," said Fuller as he smoked a cigarette this morning and watched as the swollen Thatcher Brook passed under North Main Street. "I always wanted a swimming pool."

Zac Wennburg-Smith, 15, had a more harrowing experience.

Randall Street was evacuated, forcing Wennburg-Smith to leave his residence.

"It's one I don't want to do again," he said of the experience.

Towns in the Mad River Valley also sustained major damage.

Route 100B in Moretown was still closed today as road crews assessed damaged bridges.

The first bridge north of the intersection of Route 100 and Route 100B was impassable after the approach to

Cleanup on Randall Street in Waterbury.

Route 100B just south of Moretown.

Evacuating residents on Randall Street in Waterbury.

Cleaning up silt and debris in Waterbury.

the bridge was eroded, resulting in the collapse of a large section of pavement leading to the bridge. The concrete bridge itself remained intact.

Susan Goodyear, a retired Moretown town clerk, owns an old farmhouse near the bridge on Route 100B with her sister. She has lived there off and on throughout most of her life, she said.

This morning, neighbors and friends were helping slop mud out of the house and remove damaged belongings after the Mad River rose about 5 feet up the first floor walls. Measured from the ground outside, the water line appeared to be 7 or 8 feet high.

Goodyear was heartbroken when she returned to her house.

"I cried, if you really want to know the truth," she said. "That's how it felt."

Several miles down the road in Waitsfield, a swarm of residents was cleaning out buildings at the intersection of Bridge Street and Main Street in the center of the village.

The historic covered bridge on Bridge Street was closed after being battered and bruised by the Mad River.

Waitsfield Select Board member Charlie Hosford said the damage to the bridge was superficial but added

Route 100 in Waitsfield

The Birke Photography Gallery on Bridge Street in Waitsfield.

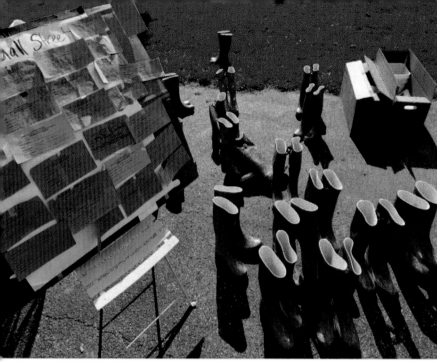

Assignments and boots wait for volunteers Wednesday after Irene.

Cleanup on Waterbury's Main Street the morning after Irene.

that it will remain closed until Vermont Agency of Transportation officials can assess the structure. There was some erosion of the abutments that support the bridge, Hosford noted.

"The bridge itself did not move a fraction of an inch," he said.

The same could not be said for a white clapboard building nearby that had been lifted from its foundation and shoved up to the edge of the road.

Other culverts and bridges along Route 100 had also washed out, and Route 100 was closed this morning south of Route 17.

Jack Carter of Waterbury helps out on Parker Court.

Volunteers (L-R): Luna Isham of Duxbury, Molly Tolland of Barre, and Sandy Shepard of Essex outside Waterbury's Wesley United Methodist Church.

The Winooski also took a toll on Richmond, one of the few towns in northwestern Vermont to be damaged. There, residents had to be rescued by kayak from their homes, 17 of which were seriously damaged.

In the town of Berlin, auto repair shop owner Brian Morse drove his backhoe into the waters to rescue residents of Weston's Mobile Home Park and their belongings, joining other rescuers in boats until the water destroyed the machine's motor.

Berlin suffered 70 of 100 mobile homes demolished, some of the roughly 170 mobile homes destroyed statewide, with others in Duxbury and Woodstock. Evelyn Holmes, 82 of Berlin, got a double-whammy. Her trailer had been destroyed in May flooding at the River Run Mobile Homes trailer park. Then the used mobile home she'd purchased at Weston's just two days before Tropical Storm Irene struck was destroyed when Irene decimated that park. Residents of these trailer parks faced not just the loss of their homes and property, but many of the trailers contained asbestos, creating disposal problems.

I GUESS I'M THE TRAILER TRASHER; BERLIN WOMAN 0-FOR-2 WITH MOBILE HOMES THIS STORMY WINTER
Published in the Rutland Herald and Times Argus on Sept. 1, 2011
By DAVID DELCORE

It's a good thing Evelyn Holmes has a healthy sense of humor, because Mother Nature sure is putting it to the test. One of a dozen residents who were washed out of River Run Mobile Home Park by late-May flooding, Holmes, 82, thought she was putting her FEMA check to good use when she found a used mobile home across town and decided to buy it.

The closing was Friday — less than 48 hours before Tropical Storm Irene unleashed its wrath on Vermont, wiping out most of Weston's Mobile Home Park, including Holmes' new home.

Different storm. Different river. Different home. Same result.

Just ask Holmes, whose belongings are still in storage — some in Barre and some in Williamstown — all ready for the move she'll never make but had planned to over the weekend.

"Same old, same old," Holmes chuckled when asked how she was doing Tuesday.

"You've heard of 'trailer trash.' Well, I guess I'm the 'trailer trasher,'" she joked, suggesting that laughing was better than the alternative.

"There's no need of crying about it," she said. "It doesn't help."

Holmes knows of what she speaks. If this were a movie, she knows how it ends. If it were a book, she's read it.

"I've seen it before," she said.

So has her daughter, Penny Peck, who along with her siblings spent the summer cleaning up Holmes' flood-damaged mobile home, which was along the Stevens Branch, hunting for the new one they eventually found not far from the Dog River, and patiently waiting for FEMA to come through with the financial assistance Holmes needed to get back on her feet.

According to Peck, things were "just starting to turn around," and her mother, who has been splitting time between Peck's home in Duxbury and her sister's home in Washington, was looking forward to moving into her own place.

"She was just so happy," Peck said. "We were all happy for her."

And then Irene arrived and it was déjà vu all over again for Holmes and her family.

"I can't believe it," Peck said. "I'm still in shock."

"She had (the mobile home) for two days," Peck said. "We hadn't even got her stuff out of storage."

That, as it turns out, may be something of a silver lining. Peck said that if her sister, Jerri Howard, hadn't driven off to Maine with the key to their mother's storage unit, the move would have started Saturday.

"Can you believe it?" she said. "She would have lost everything."

As it is, Peck said, Holmes, who hadn't yet had time to arrange for flood insurance, lost plenty — a fact she confirmed during a Monday visit to the flood-ravaged Route 12 mobile home park.

Peck said Holmes waited in the car while she slogged through oil-tainted mud to check the interior of her mother's newly purchased mobile home. Based on her experience at River Run, Peck said she had a very good idea what she'd find.

"It looked pretty much the way I expected," said Peck, describing the chaotic scene.

*There's no need
of crying about it,
she said.
It doesn't help.*

"The refrigerator was tipped over, there was mud in the toilet and tub … and the floor was all wet and starting to buckle," she said. "It's totally ruined."

Peck said she didn't take it well.

"I was just bawling," she said. "It was like: 'Here we go again!'"

Although she knew a hurricane-turned-tropical storm was headed for Vermont, Peck said she didn't think Weston's would flood. Unlike the River Run park, which is perilously close to the Stevens Branch, Weston's is a much larger park across Route 12 from the Dog River.

"(The river) had to come a long ways to do what it did," she said. "That's one of the reasons we picked (Weston's) … We thought: 'The river is far enough away, it's never going to bother her.'"

Holmes said she shared that view — until Sunday.

"Then, my goodness, Irene comes to visit and trashes my trailer," she said.

Like dozens of neighbors that she's never met and feels badly for, Holmes said she'll wait for a new federal disaster declaration and — with luck — another check from FEMA. However, this time, she said, she won't be spending it on another mobile home.

"No more trailers," she vowed. "Two trailers in three months is enough."

Given her recent run of bad luck, Holmes said she is hoping to persuade Peck to make what has been a temporary living arrangement a little more permanent.

"I'm going to sweet talk her into letting me stay with her," Holmes said.

*Different storm.
Different river.
Different home.
Same result.*

HARROWING RESCUES, THEN HEARTBREAK
Published in the Rutland Herald and Times Argus
on Aug. 30, 2011
By DAVID DELCORE

Ten days after losing her husband, Melanie Byrd may have lost her home.

Byrd waded through chest-high floodwaters to get to high ground late Sunday afternoon and was eventually carted out of Weston's Mobile Home Park on Route 12 in the bucket of a front-end loader later that evening. She spent this morning surveying the damage to her soggy double-wide.

Byrd's home, like dozens of others around it, took on nearly 2 feet of water when the Dog River ran wild Sunday — washing across a now-closed section of Route 12 and, in a startlingly short period of time, transforming the 83-lot mobile home park into ground zero in Berlin's latest flood recovery efforts.

"It happened so fast," Byrd said. "All of a sudden there was water everywhere, you could smell oil and propane, garbage cans were floating and decks were letting loose."

Byrd said she managed to get the disabled man she cares for to higher ground before her steps were swept away and her mobile home swamped.

"We stood there for what seemed like hours," she said, explaining they, and others, eventually rode out in the raised bucket of a front-end loader even as another rescue attempt went awry.

According to Byrd, firefighters were pulling a boat filled with rescued residents when they lost control of the tow rope and the boat was swept by floodwaters. Colchester Swift Water Rescue was able to assist the passengers, who were all reportedly unhurt.

Today, an emotional Byrd, who spent the night at a friend's house, was doing her best to clean up and keep it together. Mercifully, she said, the water that swept into her home spared the wooden box containing her husband's ashes, though the water came within an inch or two of the top of the table where she had left it.

Byrd, who did have flood insurance, said she was hopeful it would cover her losses, though she said she was not sure she would return to the mobile home park, much of which is in the 100-year flood plain.

"I don't know what I'm going to do," she said.

Tom Casey said Byrd had plenty of company.

"I think we're all 'former' residents (of the park)," he said, suggesting there is no fixing the damage done to many of the park's homes.

Casey, 76, said he saw the water coming and had just enough time to hop into his vehicle and drive up over a grassy knoll using an informal path the park's owner created for his tractor.

"I remember thinking: 'Here comes the water hell-bent for leather and a lot of it,'" Casey said. "I got out of here just in time."

Others didn't, according to Casey, who pointed to one stranded car that was swamped and abandoned in the middle of the road and the area at the end of Third Street where Byrd and other residents waited to be rescued.

Terry Muzzy, who owns one of roughly a dozen mobile homes atop a knoll overlooking the rest of the park, said his trailer wasn't damaged but the water threatened to crest the knoll and his family didn't think twice about evacuating.

"I've been here 20 years and I've never seen anything like it," he said.

Town Administrator Jeff Schulz, who toured the park with members of the Select Board this morning, said the damage exceeded what they saw during a similar trip to flood-ravaged River Run Mobile Home Park back in May.

Schulz estimated more than 70 mobile homes may have been substantially damaged in Sunday's flooding.

In May fewer than a dozen mobile homes at River Run — those closest to the Stevens Branch of the Winooski River — fell into that category.

Schulz said River Run and the Barre-Montpelier Road did not suffer significant damage Sunday. Instead, he said, the Route 12 corridor was hardest hit. That included Weston's, M's RV Sales and Service and a section of the state highway.

"That area really got hit hard," he said, noting Route 12 was wiped out near the railroad trestle near M's RV. A Times Argus photographer found RVs in the river and others that appeared to have been strewn in the woods. Schulz said the Select Board plans to meet tonight to determine whether to issue a temporary health order for Weston's park similar to the one that barred residents of River Run from occupying their damaged mobile homes in the wake of late-May flooding. That decision, he said, will begin a now-familiar process that will likely end with a requirement that most of the lots in the park be flood-proofed before they are reoccupied.

Ironically, Berlin's Board of Abatement was scheduled to meet today to consider the requests of a number of River Run residents that a portion of their tax bills be abated due to damage caused by the previous flood.

"Looks like we'll have to schedule another one of those (abatement meetings)," Town Clerk Rosemary Morse said.

Although several local roads were closed due to Sunday's flooding, Schulz said most were reopened this morning and three — Muzzy Road, Chase Road and Lovers Lane — were expected to be passable by the end of the day. Schulz said repairs to the lower section of Rowell Hill Road — between Route 12 and the bridge over the Dog River — will take longer.

Fire Chief Miles Silk confirmed that two volunteer firefighters were taken to Central Vermont Medical Center as a precaution after the more serious of two incidents involving rescue boats at Weston's Mobile Home Park on Sunday.

According to Silk, firefighters were using the boats to ferry residents to safety through relatively calm knee-deep water when two Northfield bridges gave way upstream, unleashing a torrent of water that changed the conditions in minutes.

"It went from knee-deep to over their heads," he said, explaining the surge spun the boat around, knocking one firefighter over and causing the other to lose his grip on the rope. The crew from Colchester rescued the firefighters — including one who was clinging to a tree — and with their assistance secured the boat, which was swept a short distance downstream.

"There were no injuries," Silk said, noting that the same was true in a second boat-related incident. Silk said a boat overturned when a resident was stepping in, and the craft was quickly flipped back over.

Addison County was relatively spared by Irene. Hancock was the only town in the county considered by state officials to be "severely impacted," while Granville, Ripton and Lincoln had moderate damage. While homes on both Route 125 and 100 had damage, the Hancock Hotel and the Vermont Home Bakery really got socked, floodwaters destroying its well and boiler.

Monday morning arrived with abundant sunshine and by Tuesday, National Guard helicopters began delivering food and water to stranded residents, but as Governor Peter Shumlin and other officials began touring the state to survey the devastation, the scope of the damage seemed almost unbelievable. Simultaneously, however, proof certain of Vermont independence was equally evident. As Wallingford Town Clerk Joyce Barbieri expressed it, "We're Vermonters. We just pull our socks up and get to work."

Rescue by backpack, golf cart, helicopter and National Guard

One of the greatest obstacles faced in reaching isolated towns and residents was the virtual destruction of so many major roads and literally hundreds of smaller ones. The old cliché, You can't get there from here, was true of dozens of communities along the central spine of Vermont and its valley communities. These towns received considerable help from the Vermont National Guard and also from units from Maine, Virginia, West Virginia, South Carolina and Illinois, from the Red Cross, the Federal Emergency Management Authority, and the State Agency of Transportation. But in the first few days, it was Vermonter helping Vermonter that made the difference.

Again, from Wilmington to Waterbury, residents took matters into their own hands, whether it was Craig Mosher and his crew rebuilding Route 4 in Killington using the very debris that Irene had moved around or local residents in Royalton who cleared a makeshift road through a sunflower field at Hidden Meadow Farm, providing access to Interstate 89. They dubbed the makeshift path Exit 2 ½, the shortest on-ramp in the country. Rachel Bigelow, who owns the farm, set up a little farm stand right there selling corn, tomatoes and flowers.

A LITTLE LESS TRAPPED
Published in the Rutland Herald and Times Argus on Sept. 1, 2011
By CRISTINA KUMKA

Craig Mosher looked up the road and saw his next job. It wasn't one he asked for. The owner of Mosher Excavating, Inc. on Route 4 in Killington has been lauded by Killington townspeople for his rapid response to historic flooding that washed out a huge section of road just north of his home and business.

Since Monday, Mosher and four of his employees, who rode into work on ATVs, have used the company's own excavating equipment to completely rebuild the road and redirect a brook into its normal path at the key intersection of Route 4 and River Road.

They've worked sunup to sundown.

Because of Mosher, more than 300 out-of-towners got out of Killington Wednesday morning and headed toward Woodstock and the interstate, and food and supplies can be delivered into town from the east.

Because of him, water isn't flowing into the Kokopelli Inn, Goodro Lumber or into the rooms of houses anymore.

Because of him, the town feels less trapped.

"I'm not a hero, I just own an excavating company," Mosher said, eating a salad for lunch as he leaned on his bulldozer Wednesday.

Mosher was given the go-ahead by the state to rebuild the road for access and redirect the brook as best as he could.

On Mosher's own property, near Blackie's store and the Irving gas station at the Killington four corners, his pasture is gone but his free-range animals are just fine.

"Big and Rib are OK," Mosher said of his two Scottish Highland cows, spreading a smile.

Mosher gave credit to the other local contractors on the other side of Route 4 doing even more work to rebuild access into and out of town - Belden and Markowski.

On Wednesday, the town of Killington announced that because of diligent road reconstruction, residents would be able to take a one-lane dirt road from Woodstock to Killington between 6:30 a.m. and 7:30 a.m. and from Killington to Woodstock between 8 a.m. and 9 a.m. beginning today and every day moving forward.

Also beginning today, The Bus in Rutland will take Killington residents back and forth to Rutland twice daily from Killington at 8:15 a.m. and 6:15 p.m.

Stops in Killington will be the Killington Grand Hotel, Pico Mountain, and Mendon Mountainview/Cortina Inn.

Beginning Sunday, there was no way into town and no way out, the result of raging water that grew in otherwise calm brooks after the area received upwards of 6 inches of rain in a 24-hour period.

The water rushed downhill to the lowest rivers and streams, taking chunks of pavement and boulders with it.

In Killington's case, it took feet of roads and a entire house.

At Pico Wednesday, horses seemed calm grazing on the wet hill behind a chair lift, now covered by 3 feet or more of mud.

Employees of the resort in charge of the horses were the opposite. They were busy figuring out a safe route to get the horses out of Killington because food and water was dwindling.

Across town on the access road, Seth Webb, the town's economic development director, was leading the charge of town officials planning where to land helicopters with food and water, how to get people medicine and how to help people in other communities like Pittsfield, which remained landlocked.

Suzie Dundas, the town's marketing manager turned co-emergency coordinator, said she's never seen a town pull together so much.

"I am shocked by the outpouring of support," Dundas said. "People have stayed for days helping people they've never met."

Steve Selbo, the developer of the town's future ski village, said he'll still invest.

Almost magically, leaders emerged in town after town where many had either recently developed emergency management plans or were in the process of doing so. Those who had been spared came forward with food and water, dry clothing and diapers, shovels and ladders, hardhats and apples, elbow grease and prayers.

By mid-afternoon Sunday, while floodwaters were still raging, the town of Wilmington's municipal water and sewer were out and people from deluged homes were taking refuge in Twin Valley High School. Residents with uncontaminated wells brought in water from their homes; others emptied their refrigerators and fed the stranded in the cafeteria. By evening, those with water were hauling the dirty dishes back home to be washed. Two nurses, Kori DeLuca and Jeannette Linnehan, quickly turned the band room into a Red Cross Center.

WILMINGTON SHOWS RESILIENCE
Published in the Rutland Herald and Times Argus on Nov. 14, 2011
By YVONNE DALEY

Susie Haughwout is no softie. After all, she's the town clerk whose car got inundated by floodwaters while she was saving the town records during Tropical Storm Irene.

But every day when she drives through the west end of town and by the former Town Office in a historic building overlooking the North Branch of the Deerfield River to her new office in a former Rite-Aid on the outskirts of tow, she just starts crying. That route takes her past some of the 48 businesses, many of them in the heart of the historic downtown, that were destroyed or badly damaged here.

Haughwout came to Wilmington in 1962 as a small child when her father started Haystack Mountain Ski Area. After college, she left Vermont to work as a legal secretary in Miami but came home in 1992 after Hurricane Andrew. She'd had enough of nature's destruction.

She became assistant town clerk in 1994 and took over her current job the next year. Now her town is reeling from overwhelming losses in both the business district and in residences, including many apartment buildings for middle- and low-income residents who can hardly afford to start over.

But even here, there's the Vermont resilience that people have been noticing since Irene. Haughwout concedes she's tired; she and her staff, along with professional movers, reconstructed the town office in just a few weeks. Since then the normal workload has quadrupled while the uncertainties have also grown exponentially.

Haughwout is not downhearted.

She points out that 10 of those 48 businesses have opened, relocated or are operating at a reduced level. And she sends out her thanks to the town of Dover, which has been helping Wilmington by paying $20,000 for an expert to assist the town with the overwhelming amount of paperwork left to be completed and another $100,000 to develop a marketing plan for the Deerfield Valley.

After Irene, the Wilmington Police and the Wilmington Town Office moved to the Shaw's Plaza on East Main Street about a half-mile from their former quarters in the center of town. It was there that Haughwout raced at daybreak Aug. 28, not having been able to sleep all night with memories of Hurricane Andrew in her mind and the Weather Channel on her television.

Wind, she kept thinking. She planned to use the building's elevator to move the town records to the second floor but she'd need the elevator to do so. The old building has very high ceilings and a handsome but steep staircase to the second floor. She feared the wind would knock out the electricity and with it the elevator. As it turned out, it was getting the hundreds of town documents and awkward, heavy equipment to the elevator that posed a problem but Haughwout solved that by using the office chairs, which have wheels, to ferry documents about.

She had elicited the help of Assistant Town Clerk Pat Johnson who brought along her friend Larry Nutting. He proved to be invaluable, moving heavy printers and other equipment by himself. Rep. Ann Manwaring, D-Wilmington, and Jim Burke, a selectman, and his wife Patti also joined in the ferrying.

Hours later, after the keys to her car came up missing and everyone but Johnson had left to try to find a way home, Haughwout went out to look at the car. It was essentially under water, Still, she thought one of the firemen could bring over the bucket loader and move the car to safety, but the bucket loader was needed to rescue people cut off by floodwaters.

"It's only a car," Haughwout says, leaving the rest of it – the greater losses in her town and the unanswered questions about the future – unmentioned for now.

Silt covers a pasture in Stockbridge.

Water covers Route 103 in Mount Holly.

Cleanup in Waterbury.

Shaw's in a tent in Ludlow.

Quechee covered bridge.

Waterbury underwater.

Route 4 in Mendon, afternoon of Irene.

HELL AND HIGH WATER: A TOUCHSTONE REOPENS IN THE TOWN HARDEST HIT BY IRENE
Published in the Rutland Herald and Times Argus on Nov. 11, 2011
By KEVIN O'CONNOR

Lisa Sullivan was off in the Bahamas last April when one of her two Vermont businesses — the Book Cellar in Brattleboro — was destroyed by fire.

"I had been sleeping for an hour," she recalls, "when I got this phone call in the middle of the night."

But Sullivan was inside her other store — Bartleby's Books in Wilmington — when flooding from Tropical Storm Irene washed away the rest of her livelihood four months later.

"We had water coming in waves," she says, "and then we smelled propane."

Owning one of Vermont's two dozen local independent bookshops is hard enough in an era of Amazon e-readers that instantly beam a world of titles for as little as 99 cents. Add hell and high water and the challenge seems crushing.

"To lose two stores to catastrophes in less than five months would be more than I could bear," Publishers Weekly blogger Josie Leavitt wrote in a column titled "Our Hearts Are Breaking." "The shock, the anger and the sheer enormity of rebuilding would have me paralyzed."

Instead Sullivan mobilized. Losing her leased space in Brattleboro, she repaired the storefront she owns in Wilmington in time to reopen for the holiday shopping season's Black Friday. Stop by the Vermont town hit hardest by Irene (more than $13 million in damage, the state says) and you'll find shelves teeming with history, mystery, romance, suspense — and one true story of resilience.

'Before I knew.'

Sullivan, a onetime West Coast software marketer, moved to Wilmington a decade ago to unplug — only to buy into her hometown Bartleby's in the spring of 2004 and Brattleboro's Book Cellar that fall.

"A really short time span," she says. "Some would argue before I knew anything."

Few shoppers seemed bothered at Bartleby's, then a still-maturing 15 years old. But many voiced concern at the Book Cellar, the most venerable store in downtown's cornerstone Brooks House. Did the new owner understand the shop was a literary landmark since Norman Rockwell appeared at its opening in 1948? That it boasted autographed photos of Robert Frost and

Dorothy Canfield Fisher? That it was one of a select few in the nation to publish its own history?

Sullivan did. She and store manager Ana McDaniel carefully stocked the historic 15-foot-high shelves reached by rolling ladders. They also attracted such national authors as Melissa Coleman, whose memoir "This Life Is in Your Hands" received a rave New York Times review just a week before a Brattleboro appearance last April 15.

The author quoted her famous gardening father, Eliot Coleman, about spring's smell of possibilities. But two nights later, upstairs apartment dwellers detected only smoke. A staple in an electrical wire had sparked a building-gutting blaze. To extinguish it, firefighters shot almost 2 million gallons of water up five floors onto the roof — and down onto the store's $250,000 inventory.

Sullivan, on vacation, watched news footage via the Internet. She could see that her landlord would need to strip the block of everything except its wooden skeleton and brick sheathing before even considering a multiyear timetable for rebuilding.

'Worst case.'

Returning to Vermont, Sullivan salvaged a few trash cans and folding chairs amid what otherwise was pulp.

"Wallowing a little bit," she recalls, "I decided I was going to take a step back and focus on Bartleby's."

Founded in 1989, the Wilmington store inherited some history when it moved from a Route 100 storefront to a 175-year-old Route 9 carriage house on its 20th anniversary. The central downtown business, with the Book Cellar's McDaniel as the new manager, enjoyed a sunny summer. Then came the forecast for Irene.

The day before the Aug. 28 storm, Sullivan was attending a family reunion in Rhode Island when her husband, Phil Taylor, suggested they return home to clear a few things off the floor.

"We were thinking, worst case, we might get an inch or two of water," she recalls.

By 8:30 the next morning, rain had swelled the nearby Deerfield River, normally 2 feet deep, to 11 feet.

Sullivan moved the store's computer from below the counter to on top of it.

Two hours later, the current, up to 25 feet, was spilling over banks and bridges.

Sullivan moved the computer to the second floor.

"We started to see the river rushing down the road."

Her husband, a carpenter, worried that outside pressure might crush the 1830s building. To save the structure, he said, they'd have to offset the strain by flooding the store.

The couple stood helpless as, opening the door, 4 feet of water gushed   inside. Smelling propane, the two then ran up the stairs, escaped out a back entrance and up a nearby hill. They had to wait two days before the National Guard let them see the loss of nearly $300,000 in stock and surroundings.

News outlets as far-reaching as National Public Radio and the Los Angeles Times reported Bartleby's flood. Sullivan, for her part, flashed back to the Book Cellar fire.

"How could I have these two things happen?"

Then she saw her good fortune.

'Who knows?'

Bartleby's was sopping but, unlike nearby buildings condemned or carried off by the water, salvageable. Touring storm-ravaged Wilmington as outgoing president of the Mount Snow Valley Chamber of Commerce,   Sullivan felt a sense of defeat morph into determination.

"I really feel we need to save this town," she says today.

Sullivan is starting with her store. Industry studies show that local independent businesses like hers reinvest almost half of their receipts back into the community — three times the figure of national chains and 100 percent more than out-of-town Internet retailers that don't pay state taxes.

Almost two dozen volunteers — "half of whom I didn't know" — began by filling Dumpster after Dumpster with hardcovers gone soft. Then came her husband and his crew with new wallboard, waterproof insulation and plans to reinforce the first floor and relocate the furnace and much of the retail space upstairs.

Sullivan is supplementing her flood insurance with a low-interest Vermont Economic Development Authority loan and a few lucky breaks. The national Borders "superstore" chain went bankrupt just after Irene, allowing her to buy $40,000 worth of its shelving for one-tenth the price. Publishers, for their part, have donated $10,000 in free product.

Bartleby's was nothing but exposed beams when Sullivan held a special leaf-peepers sale on Columbus Day weekend. As she sold books out of boxes, her 8-year-old daughter and 5-year-old son poured $661 worth of lemonade for a local flood relief fund.

Bartleby's reopened Friday when more than two dozen shoppers — some waiting outside in lawn chairs — streamed in to see neatly shelved books amid plasterboard walls and cement floors awaiting paint and carpet. (Vermont mystery writer Archer Mayor — whose latest Joe Gunther title, "Tag Man," just hit the New York Times best-sellers list — was set to visit Saturday.)

Happy ending? Not yet. Neighboring businesses such as Dot's — a diner deemed "a national treasure" by Gourmet magazine — aren't sure if they'll ever be able to return. Sullivan is equally noncommittal about the Book Cellar, whose former storefront is years away from restoration.

"Given the number of things that have happened this year, who knows?"

She's just glad to be turning a new page.

Dozens of volunteers came forward, including Abigail Howe LaVonte, 28, from Newburyport, Massachusetts. LaVonte's family goes back in Wilmington. Her great grandfather Charles Parmelee had founded a pharmacy here 104 years ago and after a fire destroyed the original building, he replaced it with a brick structure; the building near the town's center still bears the name Parmelee & Howe Building. It survived the 1938 flood but the Rev. Ralph Howe, today the pastor of Hedding United Methodist Church in Barre and LaVonte's father, recalls his father telling how the only time he'd seen his father cry was when that earlier flood washed into his new building.

LaVonte had watched the news of Irene's devastation and decided to just drive to Wilmington to try to help. She spent several days assisting Town Clerk Susie Haughwout and others in town with the clean-up.

"She drove in before the road was open," Howe said of his daughter. "My parents died in 2000 and she had such fond memories of that town. It broke her heart to see the damage. She just wanted to help."

At the Three Mountains Inn in Jamaica, emergency coordinator Paul Fraser quickly organized a response team. Volunteers showed up by the dozens. Here, as throughout the state, ATVs became essential means of transportation for checking on people cut off not just from the outside but also from the neighbor down the road. Homes in the center of town had disappeared down the river; Pikes Falls Road and the West Jamaica Road had been shattered. In town, the bridge over the Bald Mountain Brook had gone out and with it access to Route 100. But, in just eight hours or so, resident Wesley

Ameden and his crew used excavators and backhoes to put some of the river back where it was supposed to be and, where four houses had once stood along with their properties and outbuildings, Ameden constructed a new road, which for many weeks was essentially Routes 30 and 100, providing access in and out of town.

TROPICAL STORM IRENE ENDS A DREAM; A LABOR OF LOVE IS SWEPT AWAY
Published in the Rutland Herald and Times Argus on Nov. 7, 2011
By YVONNE DALEY

Tracy Payne spent the six weeks after Tropical Irene tore away her dream house picking through a debris pile downstream from where her home used to be in Jamaica. There she found, intact, a single cup from the antique china set that had been her grandmother's and her French press, also unharmed.

But where had her collection of antique guitars, her jewelry, the beautiful doorknobs she'd hunted down for her 1840 three-story house with its handsome double porches gone? And the new stainless steel refrigerator and farmer's sink, not to mention the teak and oak floors she'd installed herself? All gone.

Payne was in Boston, visiting her partner when the storm hit. Perhaps there would be some flooding in her basement if the river rose high, she thought as she heard news of Irene's damage in Vermont. Surely the second-story porch where she often sat with her morning coffee would be safe and sound.

"I got the call from the fire department. They said, 'Your house is gone,'" she recalled last week. "I said, 'Oh, maybe I can get in there and get a few things from the second floor.' 'No, really,' they said, 'your house is gone; it's gone down the river.'"

Andy Coyne had watched it go. His house, the last on Water Street, was buffeted by floodwaters, which took much of his front lawn and a row of lilac trees. Floodwaters rearranged the dirt basement and spoiled all that was down there, but his house remained intact while four others, just upstream from his, each separated from the river by expansive lawns and a road, disappeared in a matter of hours.

"It was a horrible thing to watch," he says, describing how the raging river ate away at the land, undermined foundations. Payne's house simply floated into the river, whole, then hit the bridge over Depot Street, the roof at bridge level. Coyne said it remained there a minute, then just seemed to explode, turning instantly into rubble that floated downriver.

Payne had moved to Vermont from Baltimore after 9/11, seeking a quieter life. Since buying her house in Jamaica a year ago, she had rented a home nearby so she could work on it, often putting in 14-hour days.

All the while, she was dealing with other painful occurrences – the death of a brother, her father's early onset Alzheimer's. A week before Irene, he fell and broke his back; last week, he fell and broke a hip.

Finally, last weekend, having done all she could for the time-being, she drove home to help her mom and attend a fundraiser her hometown of Fallston, MD, was having for her.
When all is settled, she doesn't plan to live in Jamaica, much as she has loved the town and people. It will be too painful. And she doesn't plan to live near a river either.

"I had my dream house for a year," Payne said.

A COMMUNITY DEFINES THE 'VERMONT WAY'
By Rep. Oliver Olsen

A year before Tropical Storm Irene swept across Vermont, I was in the midst of a tempest of an entirely different sort - an election campaign to represent the towns of Jamaica, Londonderry, Stratton, Weston and Winhall in the Vermont House of Representatives. One of my campaign advisors was a friend and veteran of the Vermont press corps, Rod Clarke. As a former journalist with decades of experience in Vermont, Clarke had bore witness to some of the seminal moments of the state's contemporary history, and brought a unique sense of Vermont's identity to the table.

So when it came time to develop a theme for my campaign, I batted around a few ideas with Rod. I had committed to running a positive campaign - a campaign of ideas, innovative thinking, and hard work; built upon the best traditions of the state I had grown up in. Rod came up with the words that went on to define my campaign: "Building a Bright Future, the Vermont Way." That message became part of advertisements, brochures and postcards in the months that followed. It was just a message, but it captured the spirit of my campaign, and I went on to win the election.

Little did I know that a year later, the people within the communities I represent would come together and define that message. In the days and weeks following Tropical Storm Irene, the actions of many gave tangible meaning to "the Vermont Way."

That Sunday morning was not unlike any other rainy morning. Everyone was expecting Tropical Storm Irene to hit that afternoon, so the patter of rain on the roof seemed like nothing more than a preview of bigger things to come. But then my wife began to notice a sound, which we initially thought was the wind. We looked out the window, and could see that the tree branches were relatively still, which further piqued our curiosity.

I went outside to investigate and quickly realized that the sound was the Ball Mountain Brook. It was similar to a sound I had heard many times before, a distant roar that was common after a hard rain, but this time the sound was much more pronounced. Something didn't feel right, and I thought it would be worth checking on the brook.

Our house is just off Route 30, a few hundred yards up the hill from the bridge that spanned the Ball Mountain Brook, at the edge of Jamaica Village. As I approached the bridge that spans the brook, the gravity of the situation came into focus. The bridge had buckled and separated into two halves under the pressure of a deluge of water that had reached the deck of the bridge; what was once the entrance to the fire station, adjacent to the bridge, had already been consumed by the raging floodwaters. The town was effectively cut off from all points north and the fire station was inaccessible.

I walked along Water Street, first on the road, and then around it. There was water running down some sections of the road, and then it came to an end. The brook had already swept away the road, the land on both sides of the road, and four homes. Just a few houses up the street from this destruction was an elderly gentleman, Fred Bement, who was watching the unfolding chaos from a chair on his front porch. I learned from his neighbor, Peter Andrus, that Fred's wife was stuck on the other side of town. Peter and I persuaded Fred and his dog to leave the house, guiding them behind some of the homes and then around an obstacle course of downed power lines, trees, and debris that the brook had tossed over the bank and onto the street.

Meanwhile, on the other side of town, the proprietors of the Three Mountain Inn, Ed and Jennifer Dorta-Duque, discovered that they were no longer running a business; within a matter of hours, their inn had become the emergency shelter and Emergency Operations Center for the Town of Jamaica. And although Fred's wife was now at the inn, there was no way to get Fred there. My next door neighbor, Margo Boyd, had taken in three other people whose homes were either flooded or unreachable, and she took in Fred while we looked for a shelter that was accessible.

I headed out of Jamaica, toward Winhall, since I had learned that they had an emergency shelter. I drove over to Rawsonville and discovered that Route 30 was impassable to Bondville, then headed north on Route 100 to South Londonderry. George Lange and his crew from the South Londonderry Fire Department had blocked off the area around the West River, which had reached the deck of the bridge that crosses the river. Debris of various forms, including propane tanks, was smashing against the bridge, and the fire house was surrounded by water. I headed over the Winhall Hollow Road to Bondville, and after a few detours, made it to the emergency shelter that had been established at the Mountain School.

By the time I made it back to Jamaica, an entire section of the bridge over Ball Mountain Brook was gone, and it was abundantly clear that we needed traffic cones and barriers - and lots of them. The sense of urgency only intensified as nightfall approached; cars, trucks, and tractor trailers were still traveling down Route 30 - trying to find a route home, but oblivious to the destruction ahead.

I picked up Fred and his dog, and we made our way to the emergency shelter in Winhall. What normally would have been a 15 minute trip took an hour. We were met at the shelter by Winhall residents Doug and Christy Mackenzie, volunteer paramedics with Londonderry Rescue, who asked what, in hindsight, should have been an obvious question a few hours earlier when Fred was leaving his home, "Does Fred take any medications?"

After a brief call with Fred's wife, they learned that Fred was diabetic and had a medicine cabinet full of medication -- back at the house.

Meanwhile, I had been in contact with the Jamaica EOC about the need to barricade the north side of the bridge over Ball Mountain Brook and the entrance to Water Street. The problem was that everything had already been deployed on the other side of the bridge. Bob Oakes, a Winhall selectman, was helping out at the Winhall emergency shelter, located an orange plastic barrel and a sawhorse, which were at the town's transfer station. I met up with Scott Bushee at the transfer station; we squeezed the barrel into the back seat of my Volvo and the sawhorse into the trunk, and headed back to Jamaica. After delivering the barricades in Jamaica, I returned to Winhall with Fred's medication.

It was about nine that evening when I made it back home. In spite of the destruction that surrounded us, all the creature comforts of home were intact. In retrospect, it seems unreal, but throughout the storm, our house never lost power, phone, or Internet service. More importantly, everyone was safe and secure that night.

Monday turned out to be a beautiful summer day that drew everyone outside. In Jamaica, Ray Ballantine erected a system of ladders that allowed people to get across the washout behind one of the abutments on the Depot Street bridge, which was downstream from the Route 30 bridge that had been destroyed. Anyone who wanted to get across town had to climb fifteen feet down one ladder, and then back up another ladder to the other side. One of the first to cross was my 93-year-old neighbor, Beverly Landman.

This was not Beverly's first experience with flooding. She grew up in Jamaica, on Water Street, and was here for the 1927 flood, the 1938 hurricane, and the 1973 and 1976 floods. Beverly spent Sunday at the home of Lexa Clark, chairwoman of the Jamaica Selectboard, who lived on the other side of town. Once the storm had passed Beverly insisted on returning to her own home. So, without hesitation, she climbed down ladder, and back up to the other side, from where she walked back home, and got to work cleaning out her flooded basement.

Shortly thereafter, Drew Hazleton and Wesley Ameden came up with an ambitious plan for a temporary road to replace the section of Water Street that had been washed away. Wesley already had his excavator in the brook by the time I crossed the Depot Street ladder detour that morning.

After reviewing the status of Jamaica's situation with the EOC, I headed over to Londonderry. The West River had flooded several businesses and homes along Route 11, including the Garden Market, Jelly's Deli, Mike & Tammy's, and Stoddard's. Fortunately, the Swiss Inn had taken in several displaced residents. The Memorial Bridge was closed due to a washout behind one of the abutments, and in the middle of Route 11, just in front of the bridge, was a deck that belonged to Mike and Ellen Carlton. The flood had taken the deck from their house and carried it down the road, where it ultimately settled. In spite of these physical obstacles, volunteers had started to emerge and the clean-up was underway.

Further upstream, in Weston, staff and volunteers had started cleaning out the basement of the Weston Playhouse. A few other basements in the village were flooded, including homes and the town office building, but the Weston Marketplace and the Weston Playhouse had taken the brunt of the storm. Flooding from the adjacent West River had flooded the basement level of the playhouse, including the kitchen, dining area, dressing rooms, and the orchestra pit. Waterlogged costumes and props for the world premiere production of *Saint-Ex* had been pulled out onto the front lawn of the playhouse, where they were being inspected and cleaned. An ambitious goal had been set: get everything cleaned up and put back together, in time for a performance of *Saint Ex* that Friday. As audacious as it was, everyone was committed to achieving the goal.

Back in Jamaica, volunteers had started to assess the destruction along Pikes Falls Road and West Jamaica Road. Entire sections of these roads had been washed away, and many areas were inaccessible on foot, let alone motorized transport. Telephone and electric service had been severed and there was no mobile phone coverage in the area. Several people were able to blaze a trail network around the worst areas and used ATVs to deliver food and water to stranded residents.

Later that afternoon, Pete Cobb and his team at Londonderry Rescue pulled together a meeting of several local emergency service agencies at their headquarters in Londonderry. I went to the meeting with Paul Fraser, Jamaica's Emergency Management Director. It wasn't until this meeting that we all had a good sense for the scale of the damage in our region. Nobody, including the Vermont Agency of Transportation, had accurate information about closed roads, the condition of roads that were still open, or detours. So, at the meeting, we developed a system where each town would send updated road conditions to the Winhall Police Department twice a day, once in the morning and once in the afternoon. The Winhall Police Department would then consolidate the information and send updates out to all the area towns - a system that proved to be an invaluable source of information in the days to come.

When Paul and I made it back to Jamaica that evening, Wesley and a crew of other local contractors had just finished roughing in the temporary road that they had started eight hours earlier. This temporary road would ultimately serve as a detour around the bridge that had washed away on Route 30, providing critical access for emergency vehicles, commuters, and tourists for the next six weeks.

It had only been a day since the storm, but the local recovery effort had already made phenomenal progress.

On Tuesday, I received a call from Wyatt Andrews, a correspondent for the CBS Evening News, who was on the road, headed toward Brattleboro. He was interested in doing a feature on Jamaica, but he and his camera crew needed to reach their satellite truck in Brattleboro with enough time to produce the story for newscast that evening. Suffice to say, Andrews and his camera crew were amongst the first to make it across the detour that had just been put in place, even though it was not quite yet officially open to public traffic.

That evening, Jamaica was the lead story on the CBS national news. What could have been another story of damage, destruction, and chaos, turned out to be one of how a community came together to overcome great adversity. Introducing his report to the nation, Andrews commented, "as impressive as the damage has been here in Vermont, today the response got more impressive." He went on to describe the recovery efforts underway in Jamaica, and reported that, "this immediate, all out effort is what residents call the 'Vermont Way.'"

By Friday, I was able to speak before a packed selectboard meeting at the Jamaica Town Hall at 6 p.m., drive through the temporary detour, across the reopened Memorial Bridge in Londonderry, and make it to Weston in time for the 7 p.m. post-Irene premiere of *Saint Ex* at the Weston Playhouse. As they say, "the show must go on." And indeed, it did.

In the days following the storm, it quickly became evident that a number of people in our community would be facing dire financial consequences. Several local residents called me up shortly after the storm and simply said, "We have to do something."

We contacted Sky Foulkes, the president of Stratton Mountain Resort, who also chaired the Stratton Foundation, a local philanthropic organization that had been co-founded by my predecessor and friend, Rick Hube. Within a few days, a massive fundraising effort had taken shape under the auspices of the foundation. The Stratton Resort emailed out an appeal on behalf of the foundation to over 20,000 of their guests. Magic Mountain did the same, and I started soliciting contributions through my constituent newsletter. Stratton Foundation coordinator Tammy Mosher helped organize fundraising events from Winhall to New York City. Thousands of dollars started pouring in, and by the end of October nearly $400,000 had been raised to help local flood victims.

Volunteers serve the National Guard in Rutland before dawn.

Dot Pingree of Plymouth surrounded by the few items she salvaged from her home.

Outside the home of Tracy Templeton in Pittsfield, defiance.

Volunteers sign up for duty in Waterbury.

Paul Fraser holds up an old photo from Jamaica that shows where four homes, washed out by floodwaters, used to be. One of those homes belonged to Tracy Payne.

In Weston, the worst damage was to the Weston Playhouse, which was celebrating its 75th season and about to have its first world premier of a musical, *Saint Ex*. More than eight feet of water had teemed into the basement, fouling everything on the bottom floor from the restaurant that overlooked the falls to recently renovated dressing rooms and the orchestra pit along with its $20,000 grand piano.

Managing Director Stuart Duke wanted to salvage the show scheduled for that Friday night, but before tackling the muck in the playhouse, volunteers from the staff helped clean mud and debris from a local store and the volunteer fire department building. As word spread of the damage to the playhouse, dozens of volunteers showed up and kept coming for days, bringing their own cleaning supplies. Local electricians replaced hundreds of circuit breakers. The green in front of the playhouse soon filled with soaked props and costumes, a virtual history of the playhouse and its performances airing in the sun. The show went on that Friday as planned, and in the next weeks, Boston's Huntington Theater solicited their audiences for financial help for the Weston Playhouse and theater alumni organized a benefit in New York City. Friends of the playhouse even donated a piano.

Wherever the storm had been, excavators proved to be necessary tools of reconstruction. Above Rutland in Shrewsbury, for example, the Cold River had overflowed its banks, demolished homes and swallowed portions of Cold River Road from the Wilmouth Hill Bridge all the way to Clarendon. The river changed course completely and had to be re-channeled back to where it belonged. Resident Judith Gould who grew up in the mountain town said, "It was a gargantuan job to dig it out with huge boulders, acres of tall trees, limbs, grass, mud and silt thrown everywhere. Even a few cars and trucks were in the mess."

Her brother Herb Carrara was the town road commissioner for years and the job was passed on to his son, Jamie. Quickly Jamie Carrara and the selectmen hired anybody who could help along with a few contractors with heavy equipment. Those men put their excavators, bulldozers and trucks into the river and started digging, putting the river back and then rebuilding the road.

"Sometimes, local knowledge works best," Gould said.

Before long, however, they were interrupted as federal FEMA officials required the job put out to bid. Still, the Vermont Department of Transportation rebuilt roads in record time, despite days of rain that returned after Irene, further complicating reconstruction and rescue efforts. To do so, the state mobilized roughly 3,000 people and more than 1,000 vehicles, about half of them private contractors.

Over and over, Vermonters compared the local response to negotiations in Washington where elected officials seemed unable to get anything done, remarking how quickly decisions on road reconstruction, distribution of goods, communication, health and human services – all the services normally associated with government – were made with little contention and no adverse impacts, at least as yet.

But Vermonters also used technology to help one another. There were innumerable websites set up – personal, municipal and public – and these, along with YouTube, Facebook and other tools brought Vermont's woes to the outside world. One of the more ingenious and useful website was #VTResponse, whose purpose was to link volunteers with people who had suffered some loss due to Irene. On its website, the organization says, "Sarah Waterman and the Reality Venture Capital team has taken on the challenge of bridging the communication gap between volunteers and those in need." Waterman got her on-the-job training in this sort of thing in Biloxi where she coordinated volunteers after Hurricane Katrina. On its website, Reality Venture Capital LLC says it "is a 2.0 beast. We operate reality television fantasy leagues and use the revenue to reinvest in New England based web start-ups."

One of the first postings on the site said, "We are looking for information from the Granville/Hancock area about people with specific medical requests, such as having prescriptions filled or over the counter drugs. There will be a group going in via bike on Saturday and they are hoping to bring items of high need to residents who may be running out of necessities." An immediate response came from someone with a horse who could help with the deliveries.

Organizers of the service were also coordinating with town clerks in Granville, Hancock, Rochester and Warren and throughout the Mad River Valley, arranging deliveries of necessities and, using the website and other means to organize volunteers. Hancock, one of those towns that had been cut off by the storm, needed it badly. Middlebury College students coordinated with #VTResponse and other organizations to bring help to Hancock, Granville and Rochester. By mid-September, more than 500 Middlebury students had volunteered nearly 2,800 hours assisting families from these Vermont towns, their efforts included delivering supplies, mucking out basements and raising funds for displaced families.

Cortney Donohue of Chester, another town that was temporarily immobilized by the storm, created a similar online community. Donohue had some previous experience with Facebook and knew its power for connecting people. She created a site called Help Vermont, and spent the days and weeks after Irene using it to solve problems. For example, a family in Ludlow wrote that their camper had been destroyed in the flood. Did someone have one they could use until October? Eric Schubert of Westminster offered his; the irony was that he knew the family in need and offered them the use of his camper. When Donohue wasn't busy monitoring the site and attending to her children, who were home from school because of the flood, she helped with the food drive in her town.

Perhaps reinforcing the notion that ordinary people could get the job done was the fact that individuals who were normally competitors quickly put aside their personal interests in the face of emergency. In Wardsboro, for example, two family-run companies that are sometimes contenders for the same contracts, Fitzpatrick Excavating and Crushing and Plimpton Excavating, came to the rescue, "They were scratching trails and pulling material where they could and accessed material locally," rather than waiting for a rescue, Assistant Fire Chief Warner Manzke said.

That happened on a larger scale when it came to state road improvements. Casella Construction, the Belden Company, Mosher Excavating and other large construction companies in Vermont that often compete for big jobs worked together to rebuild Route 4, 107 and other state highways. The scope of the projects required incredible cooperation, but cooperate they did.

Another example of initiative: On Day 2 after Irene, Central Vermont Public Service realized it could not get in to Killington to restore power on the mountain with Route 4 impassable. The utility asked permission to build a temporary road up the mountain, got it, and by the next day with the help of workmen from the Belden Company a makeshift road was in place and work on demolished transmission lines began.

And in Wallingford where flood damage occurred on both ends of town – on River Street near the village center and miles away along Route 140 where it intersects with 103, Town Clerk Joyce Barbieri was impressed by the irrepressibility of her fellow townspeople. "The people on River Street, boy were they resilient," she said of the families that had water into the first floors of their homes, several of which had survived floods in 1927 and 1976. "They shoveled the stuff out, hosed it out, tore the sheetrock out." Barbieri said the FEMA official who came to assess damage in Wallingford, "couldn't believe what they had done. He said, 'You people from Vermont are amazing.'"

Sue and Joe Duskiewicz, who live across from the Wallingford town garage, had lost their house in a fire 15 years previously, then rebuilt. That house was flooded by Irene. They lost everything on the first floor. Making matters worse, their son had been flooded out in Bridgewater. "Sue was like an Energizer bunny for the whole street. She never stopped, no one did. Sue's son had built a deck on the back of their house recently," Barbieri said. "It was like Tinker Toys. It was standing up after the flood. Someone just fixed it for her."

On the other side of town where routes 140 and 103 meet, in a neighborhood many people mistake for Shrewsbury or Mount Holly but actually is part of Wallingford, a young couple were facing problems that seemed beyond the scope of their ages. In the middle of their first season of organic farming at Evening Song Farm, in a few short hours, the rich alluvial fields that had attracted 26-year-olds Kara Fitzgerald and Ryan Wood-Beauchamp had been washed away and replaced with a morass of boulders, knots of debris and tangled wood, their summer's labor vanished.

Their CSA customers helped them clean up and the couple set to work on reinventing themselves, looking for other land to lease and exploring with mentors at the University of Vermont, where Fitzgerald had taken a course for women farmers the previous winter, on a game plan. While describing their property as a cross between a funeral home and state emergency zone, Fitzgerald showed her optimistic spirit: "It's both a setback and an opportunity to revisit our goals and dreams. Our goal when we came here was to market ourselves as people who are fully invested in the health and wellbeing of our customers and our farm. The amazing amount of support we've received makes us just want to give back and even more fully serve this community."

STORM WASHES OUT EVENING SONG FARM
Published in the Rutland Herald and Times Argus on Aug. 30, 2011
By BRENT CURTIS

The small organic vegetable farm at a scenic bend in Route 103 doesn't look like an agricultural operation anymore; it looks like a river bed. Where neat rows of crops recently stood, the Mill River now runs, and a field of flotsam stretching all the way to the highway marks the high-water mark of a flood that has effectively put the fledgling Evening Song Farm out of business.

"Leaving the farm on Sunday, watching the waves and hearing the boulders rolling, I was so sad," Kara Fitzgerald said, looking over the remains of her 3-acre farm. "It felt like my life was over. Watching this go away was like watching the last three years of our lives go for nothing."

Fitzgerald and her partner Ryan Wood-Beauchamp bought the little plot last year, borrowed a plow and seeded the land with everything from garlic and onions to apple trees and rhubarb.

The 26-year-old pair followed a calling for land conservation and community ties from their first farm in Pennsylvania to Shrewsbury where the little farm in a narrow valley of the Mill River seemed to have everything they needed.

"As soon as we saw the for-sale sign we knew it was perfect," Wood-Beauchamp said.

Following a model of community-supported agriculture, the pair quickly signed up 50 customers, donated to the local food bank and bought a booth at the Rutland Farmer's Market.

"We feel connected to where we landed," Wood-Beauchamp said. "We want to be here next year and forever."

But in the span of hours, that dream was dimmed if not snuffed out.

The Mill River, which once ran about 100 yards south of their fields behind a screen of trees, didn't just jump its banks on Sunday; the river carved a new path right through the middle of the couple's fields.

The destructive force of the torrent ripped apart the river's banks and flung large trees and boulders into a debris field covering just about all of the agricultural fields. While the river's banks were more clearly defined on Tuesday, water still spilled over much of the land, which was shorn of its topsoil.

The only area of the farm that was unaffected by the deluge was the small farmhouse and the nearby barn where recently harvested garlic hung to dry from the rafters.

The couple said they were able to save some of their equipment, including a tractor and a manure spreader but several plows were buried in the debris field and the farm's greenhouse was a twisted ruin on Tuesday.

Fitzgerald and Wood-Beauchamp said they know very little about what will happen next. They only know what they want; to farm again.

But the flood left them with more than a mess of debris to clean. With the source of their livelihood destroyed, the pair doesn't know how they will repay their debts on the land or business expenses.

Tara Kelly, executive director of the Rutland Area Farm and Food Link, said she hoped to help the pair through government relief fund; but she said that money, if available, would take a long time to acquire.

"There would be a gap," she said.

And while Fitzgerald and Wood-Beauchamp said they planned to find jobs to pay their bills, neither knows how they will be able to pay off their debts and start anew.

"There are a lot of unknowns," Wood-Beauchamp said.

But the couple is also learning they're not alone in their moment of need.

After posting dozens of pictures of the devastation on Facebook, offers of help and donations of money have poured in.

"Some people privately offered to step up. One person offered $2,000 before I came over here," Kelly said.

Fitzgerald said friends and family members are trying to use online social media like Facebook to organize and coordinate the support.

"I never felt the need to accept generosity before, but I will accept whatever is given," she said. "When you put everything into something, you don't have a lot left for anything else."

Visitors to Evening Song Farm on Facebook can see the couple's pictures and find information on how to help.

The communities of Rutland, Mendon, Killington, Chittenden and Pittsfield are connected in more ways than just geography. Lots of people live in one of these towns and work in another; elementary students from Mendon attend the Frederic Duclos Barstow Memorial School in Chittenden. With Route 4 out in both directions and surrounding side roads out as well, the kids couldn't get to school and people in Killington couldn't get groceries or medicine.

In just two days, Mendon residents took care of the problem. They transformed a once-private hiking path into a mulch-covered corridor through which as many as 1,000 people a day hiked from Killington to Mendon and down to Rutland and back again. They christened the road Wood Chip Highway. For several weeks, 33 students used the road to get to and from school every day. The New York Times called it "the I-95 of wooded paths."

Portable toilets for the hikers were donated by A1 Sewer and Drain and placed at either end of the trail as Mike Barone, Debbie Poplawski, Al Wakefield, Jennifer and Fred Bagley, Chris Kirbach, Darrin Snitker and dozens of other volunteers manned tents where adults and kids could fill up on water, donuts and gummy bears, and should they wish get a ride a half mile from one end of the trail to the other on golf carts donated by the Green Mountain National Golf Course. And on either side of the trail, volunteers waited to drive the stranded to Rutland or to Killington and beyond.

Janice VanDyke, who lives near the forest trail in Mendon, made 50 trips up and down the mountain in the first few days, bringing back food and medicine and reuniting families. Indeed, she spent so much time yelling directions to people who were coming out of the woods and trying to find their way to civilization the day after the storm that she lost her voice.

Meanwhile, members of the Chittenden Fire Department were doing all they could to get help and supplies to people along Route 100 in Pittsfield and Stockbridge. Over the course of 15 days, volunteers delivered 120 truckloads of needed water, food, medicine and supplies in an emergency caravan to Pittsfield and Stockbridge. Some of the volunteers hiked in water, food and diapers to residents trapped deep in the woods and on back roads. Jan Sotirakis, one of the volunteers, was especially concerned about those who had mortgages and had lost their homes. She and the other volunteers raised $38,000 in the weeks after the flood but pointed out that much more would be needed, especially for families like one she knew in Rochester whose bank took their $120,000 insurance reimbursement to pay off the mortgage.

CUT OFF BUT NOT ALONE
Published in the Rutland Herald and Times Argus on Sept. 6, 2011
By ROB MITCHELL

While National Guard choppers drop pallets of MREs and bottled water into isolated towns like Pittsfield and Stockbridge, a string of resupply convoys by the Chittenden Volunteer Fire Department have provided beyond the essentials in a citizen-organized model of on-the-fly logistics. The effort has only strengthened ties between the communities that share mutual aid agreements and a web of connections among relatives and longtime friends.

The CVFD effort began in earnest when Jan Sotirakis flagged down CVFD Chief Scott Poljacik on Monday night.

"She said, 'I feel like we've got to do something,'" Poljacik said. "I was like, absolutely. And she just went with it."

The Fire Department held a meeting Tuesday night, and on Wednesday the first four trucks went up the barely passable road into Pittsfield. Thursday, Friday and Saturday 10 or 11 truckloads a day went up. By Saturday the convoy went through Pittsfield and on to Stockbridge.

The volunteers have been coordinating with the Killington command center and Restoring Rutland; the Barstow PTO and the Mountain Top Inn have contributed meals and drinks. The outpouring of support has been unbelievable, Sotirakis said.

"People have just driven up and dropped off checks - we've had at least four checks for $500," she said.

"We just got asked - they needed four cots and portable radios," she said, pointing to folding cots and boxes in the bed of one truck. "And we got them, right away."

Any money left over will go to the Pittsfield department's depleted budget. The donations go to fulfill requests from up on the mountain, which have come over cellular networks via Facebook.

"The cell phone has been absolutely crucial, between Facebook and just having cell communication," said Josh Merrill, one of the Chittenden convoy volunteers. "For the first three or four days, that's absolutely how the communication happened - by Facebook on mobile phones."

He stopped a moment to reflect.

"Two years ago this would not have happened," he said, because people didn't have smart phones with Facebook apps on them. But, "it goes a lot deeper. You have to have friends to even make the connections. It's not enough to just have Facebook."

Connections like Merrill's cousin, Brian Merrill, a Pittsfield Volunteer Fire Department officer. Brian Merrill and his fiancée, Del'Rae Merriam, have been busy organizing requests to send to Chittenden and resupply efforts farther along to Stockbridge.

Merriam - and many in the town of Pittsfield - have been deeply moved by how the town has pulled together and how their neighbors over the mountain in Chittenden have come through.

"The town could not be thankful enough for Josh Merrill and the CFD, we have so many comforts," Merriam said.

The effort has deeper meaning as Brian Merrill and the fire department contemplate the road ahead.

"It's gonna be a long winter," Merrill said, taking a break for a moment. "We've got people worried about making car payments, mortgage payments, people who can't get to work."

The threat of rain coming Sunday night was enough to make several people tear up at the thought, but the CVFD convoy is one of the things that sustains them.

"Every day they've been rolling in with these trucks," Brian Merrill said. "It's amazing."

Saturday's convoy set off from Chittenden behind a red GMC Sierra driven by Chief Poljacik with Debbie Ellison riding shotgun. Nine pickup trucks and an SUV were strung out behind, driven by volunteers like Doug Todd, George Herrick and Nicole Ferrell-Moorehouse, who had returned to her native town from New York to join the effort. They all flew small American flags taped to antennae as identifying markers.

A woman stopped work on her stone wall to stand up and watch. As the convoy entered Pittsfield, people stopped work to clap and cheer. Some walked up when the convoy slowed down and grasped hands with the drivers, shared a laugh or a smile, and said: "Thank you."

The convoy continued north into Stockbridge, at several points passing through a path plowed through a 4-foot high riverbeds of gravel, stones, mud and trees cast across Route 107 by small rivulets that had turned into raging torrents on Sunday night. A work crew was cleaning out the Stockbridge town office, leaving a plume of mud in the parking lot and furniture in the sun to dry. The town sign, and the office, had been relocated across the road and uphill to what had been Teeny Tozier's Restaurant, which opened earlier that summer.

At Stockbridge Central School, the convoy backed up to the doors, where teams of volunteers made a chain to pass supplies - toilet paper, detergent, water, food, rakes, and more - into the tiny school common room. Inside, supplies were stacked chest-high with narrow aisles for navigating between them. Despite the abundance, organizers were thinking long term - Route 107 between Stockbridge and Bethel is completely wiped out, making a trip into a grocery store an adventure. The school has become a food shelf, and the CVFD a lifeline.

As the convoy packed up to go - with Josh Merril making last arrangements to coordinate road crews - the Stockbridge residents stood and cheered.

On the way back, they stopped by Pittsfield to collect a Vietnamese pot-bellied pig - "Princess Pancetta" - that needed to be evacuated, and were flagged down by a man who had just tripped while cleaning his house and badly gashed his hand on broken glass. He joined them for the ride out, his hand held high.

People have just driven up and dropped off checks - we've had at least four checks for $500.

National news media covered the story of newlyweds Marc Leibowitz and Janina Stegmeyer of New York City, stranded Sunday along with members of the wedding party and dozens of their guests, after floodwaters swamped the couple's honeymoon cottage. The honeymooners narrowly escaped in a four-wheel-drive rental car just before a bridge behind them collapsed. Private helicopters airlifted more than a dozen of the 60 or so guests out on Tuesday, but most of the guests pitched in to help around town.

The better story, however, didn't make the national news. Brian Merrill and his fiancée Del`Rae Merriam had spent 15-hour days during the week and a half after the storm organizing emergency services in town when they should have been planning their own wedding at the Summit Lodge, scheduled for September 10. Working with the Chittenden Volunteer Fire Department and local volunteers, Brian Merrill helped organize rescue missions all over Pittsfield and into neighboring Stockbridge while Merriam made sure residents were fed and cared for. When it became apparent that they couldn't get to the Summit in Killington and that most of their guests couldn't get there either, the couple decided to throw a wedding barbecue on the Pittsfield green and invite the town.

Within a day of that decision, however, town residents had reciprocated with their own gift. Courtney and Joseph Desena, who own the Riverside Farm, a popular wedding site, had postponed a wedding planned for their inn and offered their beautiful grounds and facilities to the Merrills. Soon the Swiss Family Inn was offering to help with food and the event had become an opportunity for the town to celebrate what they'd been through together and to thank Brian and Del`Rae Merrill for all they'd done for their fellow Pittsfield residents.

Jeremy Prior, one of the volunteers who'd backpacked food and water into stranded residents of nearby Stockbridge, called the couple, "our rocks. They were so well organized that it made the rest of our jobs easy."

Brian Merrill shrugged off the compliments. "One person couldn't have done it without everyone working together, without putting any differences aside and working together," he said. "This town will never be the same. It will be 10 times stronger than ever."

By differences, he was referring to the normal kind of tension that often occurs in small towns between long-settled families and newcomers, especially newcomers with a lot of money. Millionaire trader and Spartan Race founder Joe Desena and his wife had raised eyebrows when they began purchasing properties in town and turning several into wedding and tourist facilities that were rather extravagant. It wasn't just their generosity during the storm that brought down barriers between the new and long-term residents, but also their willingness to roll up sleeves and get into the business of carting off debris and rebuilding roads.

> ## PITTSFIELD COUPLE MAKE IT A TOWNWIDE WEDDING
> **Published in the Rutland Herald and Times Argus on Sept. 12, 2011**
> *By YVONNE DALEY*
>
> Rather than light one candle from two, as is often the custom in wedding ceremonies, Brian Merrill and his wife Del`Rae Merriam Merrill poured sand from two vessels into one. Pastor Howard Gunter said the sand could never be unblended, unlike wedding candles extinguished at the close of the ceremony. "That's flood sand," Brian Merrill joked and the crowd of more than 120 neighbors, friends and family members filling the

Pittsfield Federated Church on the town green joined in the laughter.

For the past two weeks since Tropical Storm Irene made the town of Pittsfield a battered island, isolated on both ends by ravaged roads and leaving at least nine families homeless, the couple has spent long days organizing the town's emergency services rather than planning for their wedding.

Day after day, for 12 to 15 hours, they checked on the stranded and made sure supplies and food got distributed not just here in Pittsfield but in neighboring towns like Stockbridge and Rochester that were also devastated by the storm and its flood waters. By late last week, it had become clear that their wedding planned for the Summit Lodge in Killington was not going to happen.

Not only would be it nearly impossible to get themselves and their out-of-town guests there, but Brian Merrill, 35, was an officer on the Pittsfield Volunteer Fire Department as were many of his groomsmen. After what they'd been through and more still to go, with many roads still inaccessible, leaving Pittsfield was no longer an option.

By Thursday, they were planning a town barbecue, but the town wasn't letting them get off that easily.

In stepped Sharon Mayer, a wedding planner from Pittsfield who offered her services, and Courtney and Joseph Desena who own the Riverside Inn, a popular wedding site. The Desenas had postponed a wedding planned for their inn and offered their beautiful grounds and facilities to the Merrills. Soon the Swiss Family Inn was offering to help with food and the event had become an opportunity for town residents to show the Merrills how much they were appreciated and for the Merrills to share their wedding with their neighbors.

"It was just like them," said Mayer, clipboard in hand. "Here they'd done so much already for the town and they decided they didn't want to leave here for their wedding. They wanted the town to be part of it. They were going to barbecue on the green but the town decided they should have the wedding they had planned."

And they did. Del`Rae Merrill got to wear the beautiful gown with its long flounced skirt and form-fitting bodice and Brian wore a handsome black suit with white tie and vest, his children Madison and Wyatt by his side. Six groomsmen in black with red vests and ties, most of them volunteer firemen from town, and six bridesmaids in long black dresses and carrying bouquets of local sunflowers and hydrangeas, flanked the couple as Gunter read from the Song of Solomon which includes the words, "the rains are over and gone."

The couple rode to the Riverside Inn in the town fire truck while the wedding party and the couple's parents were ferried there over a hastily rebuilt bridge in a hay wagon pulled by a tractor.

Before long, members of the Chittenden Volunteer Fire Department had shown up to offer their congratulations. The two departments have worked closely together since the flood. Ben West, Chittenden assistant fire chief, said his department had delivered 100 loads of supplies to Pittsfield, Stockbridge, Killington and Mendon by Saturday.

While many talked about the wedding symbolizing a new beginning and an appropriate thank-you to the Merrills, they were quick to praise others, people like Mel Colton, 83, who has spent the last two weeks working 10 hours a day on the roads and in driveways with his excavator.

"It's what I do," he said humbly. "I've been working since I was 8 years old. I'm never retiring."

Gavin Curtis, 11, of Rochester, carried food into Tom Wicker, a retired New York Times journalist who lives in town; Jeremy Prior and Sean Krevetski backpacked 60-pound loads of water into Stoney Brook Road, a section of Stockbridge that has been cut off since the storm.

But as Prior put it, Brian and Del`Rae Merrill "were our rocks. They were so well organized that it made the rest of our jobs easy."

Brian Merrill shrugged off the compliments. "One person couldn't have done it without everyone working together, without putting any differences aside and working together," he said. "This town will never be the same. It will be 10 times stronger than ever."

As for a honeymoon, he said, "We've had it the past two weeks on Pittsfield Island."

Brian and Del`Rae Merrill's wedding was a town event, a celebration of surviving Irene and rebuilding their community.

THE NEW NORMAL: ISOLATED TOWNS SETTLING INTO LIFE AFTER IRENE

By Rob Mitchell,
State Editor

By Thursday after Irene, children in Pittsfield had learned to tell the difference between a Chinook and a Black Hawk helicopter by listening to the sound of the rotor blades overhead.

In Stockbridge, locals traded tips on the tastiest Meals Ready to Eat with rescue workers and Forest Service personnel as they took a break from off-loading supply trucks.

Irene has thrown groups of residents, volunteers, rescue workers and state emergency crews together into temporary communities born of necessity, where strong bonds are formed quickly but nothing is as it was before the storm.

Traci Templeton stood Friday next to her ruined house and boxes of rescued photographs, clothes and papers, answering questions from Rep. Peter Welch.

"I'm very fortunate. I have my past," she said. "(My daughter's) baby photos, her baby clothes. Winter stuff was upstairs. I have winter stuff."

Peter Borden, Pittsfield's emergency management coordinator, has been fielding calls from the national media for days on any one of three cell phones he carries in his car, while organizing volunteer repair crews for washed-out roads, supply runs to Stockbridge and rushing south of town to meet a Chinook helicopter dropping off shrinkwrapped pallets of bottled water and MREs.

Under the eaves of the Pittsfield General Store, he thanked a camouflage-clad soldier wearing the patch of the 101st Airborne Division, who had arrived in a chopper to pick up a sick resident.

A dozen children were playing in the playground out back of the Town Hall, while a group of men barbecued pizzas on the town green. ATVs and rugged golf-cart-like vehicles called Gators carried people and supplies from point to point.

Patty Haskins, the town clerk, answered a phone call Thursday.

"Hello, Town of Pittsfield." Pause. "I'm sorry, the town is in a state of emergency. Can you call back in two weeks?"

The caller, undeterred, tried to find out about a tax payment, but Haskins put him off to return to organizing the town's resources.

Millionaire trader and Spartan Race founder Joe Desena drove by in his backhoe, unshaven and smiling. He picked up a pile of ruined carpet in the bucket and carried it down to the mud-covered parking lot of Pittsfield's Bikram Yoga studio, where he dumped it into an oversize trash container. Casella was scheduled to make its first trash pickup later Thursday.

Both Stockbridge and Pittsfield had enough food and clothing delivered by the middle of the week. But a host of issues remain — electricity and phone service is slowly coming back on line, but the cleanup and rebuilding of severely damaged roads has just begun.

One small cluster of houses above Stockbridge, on Stony Brook Road, is completely isolated, and will not be reconnected for months, said Detective Sgt. Eric Hudson of the Vermont State Police on Thursday.

"We found out late yesterday that the road into those folks is not going to be completed until next spring," he said. "The significance of the washout, the amount of resources that it would take would be too significant at this point because of the road structure, getting heavy trucks in here is weeks and weeks away."

He said Route 107 through Stockbridge, which in places has been completely carried away, was two to three weeks from having a temporary roadbed that would allow heavy equipment and supply trucks in.

However, Jane Eubanks, a resident of Stony Brook Road, said Friday that the town highway department in Stockbridge had told her that her road would be "passable and plowable by the time snow flies."

"I do know at least two of the men (who live above us on Stony Brook Road) are earth-moving people and they're already building the road," she said. "We're pretty tough. After the flood, we dragged up a cooker and smoker and just had camp cooking."

Robin Crossman, a veterinarian and finisher of Pittsfield's notorious Death Race earlier this year, was on a mission to find a 17-year-old cat trapped in a house.

"A woman called in about her cat holed up in her house high above Pittsfield," he said. "She stopped by the clinic with her house keys and directions, and asked for an extraction."

He rode up with Bradford Broyles, the Rutland County GOP chair, who was delivering water, medical supplies, pet food and a hand-written note to someone in town. They stopped at the town green and Crossman offered advice to a man about his dog. A woman had asked them to evacuate her pet Vietnamese pot-bellied pig, but they were unable to locate her. Their search for the cat carried them up a muddy, undermined road high in the hills, and ultimately ended with the 17-year-old Nala meowing in a cardboard box in the back of the SUV.

A caravan of a pickup truck and two heavily laden sedans made their way north to Stockbridge with supplies. Route 100 was washed out in several places, and the bridge across the White River near Ted Green's Ford — which was rebuilt just recently — was buckled and undermined on the north side. A field of corn beside the river was bent as if blown by a heavy wind, but still standing.

The convoy arrived at Stockbridge Commons and unloaded its supplies into the basement of the commons meeting house, where fire crews and rescuers had gathered to coordinate.

"Even within little remote communities of four houses, they're banding together. It isn't easy," said Bethel Fire Chief David Aldrighetti in a gravelly, powerful voice. "You know, we've got a long, lonely haul ahead of us, that's for sure."

Since Monday, Aldrighetti had been evacuating sick or elderly residents, getting people out of washed-out areas, and delivering medical supplies and food to remote areas, via back roads up from Bethel.

"This is worse than anyone anticipated," said Pat Edwards, of White River Valley Ambulance. "You do feel bad. I've got some friends who have lost everything."

WRV crews had been involved in many rescues and evacuations, she said, including a rappel over a washed-out section of Route 12A from the top of a Randolph Center Fire Department ladder truck to evacuate two elderly ladies "... and then get probably a dozen other folks who just didn't want to stay on that newly formed island up there any more."

Pittsfield homeowner Brian Halligan surveyed the damage to his home just off Route 100 south of town.

"FEMA's not gonna put a dent in what it cost me," he said. "FEMA's 30,000, that's all. It's nothing. I can't pay a mortgage. It's nothing."

Even with little remote communities of four houses, they're banding together. It isn't easy. You know, we've got a long, lonely haul ahead of us, that's for sure.

In Rochester, it was immediately apparent there would be no electricity, phone service or access out of town for days. The needs were many. Twenty homes were severely damaged; eight were destroyed or close to unlivable. With freezers thawing and food spoiling, the Huntington House staff prepared a community supper for residents and served it outside. Quickly, twilight community suppers became almost a daily ritual as the Huntington House, The Café and Mac's Valley Market gave food away; Sandy's Books & Bakery turned into a kind of open-door soup kitchen.

Under any circumstances, Sandy Lincoln's café and bookstore, housed in a pretty Victorian painted lemon and lime, offers creature comforts with its yummy food and pastry, and the quirky collection of new, old and rare books, housed in five rooms where customers can chat over coffee or eat lunch; blown glass balls and "silkscapes" hang in the windows. In the weeks following the storm, Sandy's café morphed into a sanctuary where those who had lost their homes could rest, leave and receive messages, and fuel up. Employee Ruthellen Weston, who was stuck in Rutland, spread news about Rochester to the outside world on a Facebook page while Lincoln made soups and salads from her garden, which had been unharmed. Over the course of the first few weeks after the storm, residents from the village and far-flung enclaves of town would wander in, some of them shell-shocked from the damage, and found a welcoming setting.

In those first days, ATVs became a means of transportation as residents ferried supplies to those who couldn't be reached otherwise. Cell service could be found only at a spot on the top of Bethel Mountain; residents made that trek on a daily basis to get word out to worried friends and relatives, sometimes creating a caravan up the long, twisty road out of town.

Friends and generous souls, along with gawkers, found their way to Rochester, pitched in on the clean-out, brought newspapers and other vestiges of the outside world. They got there by foot, mountain bike, back-country motorcycles and ATVS. Baba-a-Louis bakery in Rutland sent 100 loaves of bread to Rochester by back roads.

Lincoln's friends, Beth Frock and Jon Graham, were among those who lost their homes. The three-story farmhouse they and their two children had lovingly filled with their own collection of rare books and art, souvenirs from their lives abroad and travel, and family photos were swept away when what was normally a very small stream eroded the little hill their home was built upon and it collapsed. Graham, a writer and translator who grew up in Rutland and is the acquisitions editor at Inner Traditions, a Rochester publishing venture, had gone back into the house to gather some documents when it went down, a falling bookcase saving him from harm. The family moved into Graham's mother's house nearby. She had died the past winter; her library of books was lost in Graham's home, too. Although the family had shelter, how strange it seemed to Graham to be almost moving backwards; the loss of the house and the family's possessions, after the recent loss of his mother, and the need to provide stability to the children made the next weeks all the more painful. Still, Graham didn't complain, except maybe about the insurance company that declined his claim. Rather than dwell on his losses, he joined others in the clean-up, as did his wife.

"It's been a major blessing how supportive the community continues to be," Graham said a few weeks after the storm. "Insurance is supposed to be there for you – you pay your premiums or else – but when it's their turn to do right, they weren't there. But the people who came to help were a blessing. Vermont is unlike any place we've ever been," he said.

REBUILDING
By Jon Graham

The last two months have been defined by the death of our house – a death that mirrored the loss of my mother nine months earlier. The holistic vision we had of our life has become fragmented and everything has to be dealt with separately – in neatly compartmentalized pieces. We sometimes no longer recognize the picture of our house lying in pieces across the streambed, as if it had been a card castle, which still pops up in newspapers and on the television. We resist the power of that image out of fear it will steal the place of the home we once had, a home that was full of friends, books, and art, and powerful memories. A home that both our daughters had grown up in and was the traditional site of the family Christmas. We loved its location next to the small stream that wound gently through its tree covered banks and where our daughter Chloe would catch trout from the pool beneath a small waterfall every spring.

Ironically our beloved home was destroyed by the rain-swollen waters of that same stream that normally struggles to reach ankle level in the late days of August. For hours preceding the final collapse of our home we were paralyzed witnesses to the relentless force of the water flowing below our deck. The destruction was swift. The raging stream first methodically took down each and every one of the trees that lined the bank along the stream bed some four feet away from the back of the house, which stood safely, so we thought, some eight feet above the torrent. Once the trees were gone, the bank began surrendering to the water, necessitating a quick and risky dash to turn off the propane tank before the stream carried it off. The events that followed occurred in quick succession over the space of an hour. Never during that time did we fear that our house would be destroyed – our neighbor's house, which was lower and whose basement was already full of water, seemed to be in much greater danger. It seemed only a matter of time before his foundation would be completely undermined by the unrelenting force of the water. But the unimaginable proves to have a way of becoming real.

The first sign of the death of our house was the swift erosion of four or five feet of ground beneath the deck. It was suddenly suspended in mid-air with the four white concrete pylons that had formerly anchored it into the ground dangling freely. One soon snapped and fell into the water, bobbing along the surface as if it were made of Styrofoam until it vanished from sight on the other side of the Rte 100 bridge. I remained convinced the house was high enough to avoid being flooded but it was soon evident that the deck's absence allowed the water to directly strike the corner of its foundation. The house may still have withstood that assault but the sudden collapse of the retaining wall along the stream bank made it possible for the river to start carrying off the ground beneath the house—in quantities far greater than any excavator could manage. The air became pungent with the heavy aroma of wet soil. It was at this point that my wife Beth, more prescient than I, told our daughters to pack bags with a change of clothes and to get their most valuable items and go to the neighbor's up the road. Those same neighbors and I began moving the furniture and other items from the rooms overlooking the stream into the front of the house so as to put less stress on the compromised foundation. (This proved fortuitous as the dining room table became wedged across the dining room doorway, therefore preventing some things from falling into the stream – but we would only discover this two days later when we were able to get back into the house.) While doing this, we heard a large rumble from beneath our feet and my eldest daughter, Rhianna, came running in to say that all of "grandma's book were floating away." My neighbor Ed and I went downstairs to find that the entire back wall of the basement had been pulled away and water was now splashing through the basement whose floor had clearly started to subside.

It was time to abandon the house, but my wife and I went back in to find our cats at the urgent request of our daughters. Still thinking that the house was not in imminent danger of complete collapse, we looked under beds and in closets in all the rooms on the second and third floor. We found one of the two cats, which Beth promptly took to the neighbor's house across the road. Our search for the other was fruitless until about two minutes before the house collapsed, he popped out of hiding clearly ready to leave. I remained on the second floor for a moment to grab Chloe's beta fish bowl, when Beth called for me to come down and help get the cat into the carrier. As I headed down the stairs, she gave up that notion and saying, it's time to get out of here, clasped the cat tightly to her chest and headed out. I was ready to follow her out the door, when out of the corner of my eye I noticed the bag I had backed with valuable papers and my laptop sitting in the chair. Still clutching the doorknob, I leaned back to snag the strap of the back, and I just kept going.

On learning that I was in the house when it toppled backward into the stream, most people ask if I was terrified. Oddly enough, the answer is no. My initial sensation as I was violently tossed back from the front of the house toward the kitchen was simply an emotionless blur. It was as if the speed of the event was too fast for the formation of any feeling in response to it. While lying on my back semi-stunned, aware that the water was swiftly creeping up my legs, my first thought was: So this could be the end of my story. This thought did not scare me so much as prompt a kind of tranquil acceptance. This was followed by the idle thought: I'm not seeing my life flash before my eyes. And then a kind of cool focused consciousness took over that methodically told me what I needed to do to get free of the debris (wriggling out of my coat for one thing) and twisting my way forward toward the door. I realized that the rubble that covered my legs had been diverted by the large book case in the hall, which was too tall to fall flat upon the floor, and it had in fact formed a cave that provided a haven from the plaster and boards falling from the ceiling, which given the importance of books in my life I found rather appropriate. I was also thankful I had not been knocked senseless by a copy of the Club Dumas, and briefly struck by the strange nature of the human mind that would create thoughts like that in such dire circumstances. But that passionless state of mind was necessary for me to focus solely on the most efficient way to get out of a house that I could hear was still being torn open by the water. Though I was crawling through the wreckage of things valuable to me, none of it made any impression that could deflect my attention from the front door and the voices of my neighbors offering support. I do not clearly remember pulling myself upright and lurching onto the porch, where our former neighbor Sean was waiting with his hand outstretched to pull me over the fissure that now gaped between our porch and the foundation wall. It was also thanks to his guidance that I was able to get out as quickly as I did. Our house had cracked from its foundation and fallen into the hole that had once been the hill on which it stood. Seconds after I emerged, the third floor separated with a large crack from the body of the house, which subsided deeper into the stream.

After the idea of my death subsided, the "what ifs" surfaced and began crowding my thoughts. Although I was not lucky enough to avoid going down with our house (like the captain in his ship), if the house had fallen a minute sooner while I was still upstairs, I think my chances of pulling myself out would have been greatly reduced. I also ruefully contemplated the paralysis that had taken hold of me earlier that afternoon and robbed me of my ability to make decisions. The thought that our house would enjoy the same fate as the trees that formerly lined the stream was inconceivable. In hindsight I can see that I was in a profound state of denial and that were it not for my wife's realization of the gravity of our situation, the odds are good we may all have been in the house when it fell. Choices that had seemed inconsequential at the time proved to have life and death significance.

My escape from the house resembled a rebirth – and I had a fleeting thought about the tomb or womb metaphor I could spin from that. My chief thought— looking for any kind of silver lining – was that at least almost losing my life put the whole event into the proper perspective. My neighbor, Robert, whose house would be saved by the destruction of ours, was among the first to come up and tell me how sorry he was. I responded that it was all just stuff. More important was embracing my wife and daughters who had seen the house go over while I was still inside and had thought the obvious.

But all those things I had blithely written off as just stuff turn out to have much deeper roots in our psyches then I initially realized. These things we collect around us, both by design and by chance, both consciously and obliviously, serve in fact as reference points charged with memory. They provide compass points for the orientation of our daily lives. I have come to realize that they form a hierarchy of values. The things that are rare and irreplaceable have stronger connections than the merely practical, but there is no hard fast rule – my mother's ancient spatula older than I am was just as valued as the African mask I found at a flea market for $50 and later found to be worth thousands of dollars. Then there are those things you only realize are missing when you reach for it to perform a routine task and you are again confronted by the absence of yet another thing that has gone with the water.

But there are some things that have a deeper claim on our inner lives – the photos of family and friends of course, but also in my case, books and art works by the many people who have been my friends. I again felt all the pain I felt on learning of my friend Radovan's death on Christmas of 2009, when I discovered that some of the copies of his books he had personally dedicated to me – with his unique multicolored dedications – were among the many things we lost.

We did not lose everything, some things were salvaged from the wreckage – although some of them turned out to be beyond rescue and repair, there was a kind of solace to be had in seeing them and knowing they were gone. And the river has surrendered some of what it carried away – school photos, a painting, a rocking horse, some African and Mexican masks are among the items people found on the banks and returned, some as far as two miles downstream. This carries its own kind of dilemma; it gives hope that other things might turn up, obscuring the potential lesson from the whole experience on reducing the hold we allow our possessions to have on us. A friend asked me what I miss most, the answer changes every day. There are a few items, some mine and some belonging to other members of my family, which I would dearly love to see return. But beyond the sentimental musings the memories of the things we lost inspire, the underlying truth reemerges: it is still just stuff. Some of it quite valuable, some easily replaced, but all reduced to the same state by the relentless activity of the water. Life has moved elsewhere. But what I do miss most is not so much our house but the belief I once had that "a man's house is his castle." Things seem more transient now, and I feel less secure. This can be attributed in part to post traumatic stress; for a month I had to deal with abrupt fears that the house I was in was tilting to one side, or vivid dreams centered on raging waters and collapsed homes. And additional stress comes with the fight to put the pieces back together. The generosity of individuals has not been matched, unfortunately, by all the institutional entities that allegedly have our backs when dealing with things like this. (I must make clear not to include FEMA in this latter category as it has been extremely supportive.)

But this unstinting generosity of friends and neighbors and family has been a consistent source of strength. From the women who painted the bedrooms in the home where we are now staying to the friend who replaced – for free – a print my daughter Chloe had in her room and listed as one of the ten things she missed most, we have been blessed by the knowledge that an enormous number of people are willing to sacrifice their time, energy, and even money to help us back onto our feet.

Life has become pre-Irene and after-Irene. An event like this seems to hold its own with such traditional life-changing rites of passage like moving away from home or getting married. However it may be even more powerful because it is not anticipated. It seems to dwarf the transitional events of a regular life. But it is also an event that is both traumatic and cathartic. It is a deep wound that carries the source of its own healing. Ultimately what we lost, such as that sense of security that our lives will unfold exactly as we plan, becomes an invitation to deep reflection and a reevaluation of one's life. An event like this shatters the assumptions our lives are based on just like the water destroyed the foundation upon which our house once sat. It overturns the notions we once held about life and death and what had been unimaginable allows us to see things on the horizon that had been previously invisible. While the storm succeeded in taking away the house and the life it represented from us, it did not take away the spirit within that allowed us to build that life. That spirit remains and we can draw on its strength to rebuild.

Students say the Pledge of Allegiance at Killington Elementary School on their first day back.

One of the most disturbing problems in Rochester, of course, were the coffins that had been washed out of the Woodlawn Cemetery, some spilling their remains along the river. Some of the graves were quite old, making identity difficult. Tom Harty, a former state trooper and funeral home director from Randolph, came forward to lead the recovery of the remains. LaShare Edwards, a registered nurse and part-time resident of Rochester, joined Harty, Selectman Doon Hinderyckx and other volunteers to do what they could with the scattered bones and coffins until federal specialists arrived to help.

Sue Flewelling, a member of the cemetery board, says it broke her heart to meet and talk with relatives of people whose remains had been disinterred. Flewelling lives off Route 73, a section of Rochester reached by a bridge across a branch of the White River, a bridge that collapsed under the force of floodwaters. After a few days, residents fashioned a footbridge over the river with fallen trees and lumber, replacing the previous means of travel by small boat. Day after day, mothers and fathers pushed strollers over the bridge and residents used pushcarts to bring groceries home. The full stretch of Route 73 from Rochester to Brandon remained closed until November 8.

Restoring Rutland — another example of community spirit and munificence, Vermont style — was the brainchild of a citizens group organized by Jim Sabataso, Katye Munger and other young people. Working with the Chittenden Volunteer Fire Department, Doug Casella of Casella Construction, and students from Castleton State College, the volunteers gathered and distributed food and supplies to isolated communities all along Route 100, using a loose network of friends connected by old-fashioned word-of-month and social media tools like Facebook.

These volunteers, primarily young adults, set up a storefront at 34 Strongs Avenue under The Palms restaurant in downtown Rutland, amassed and packaged a formidable supply of food, diapers, candles, clothing and flashlights, all the things one might need after a flood. Then they coordinated with Chittenden firemen, Casella and a convoy of volunteers, sometimes using ingenious routes and means, including backpack and ATVs, to get the goods into Killington, Pittsfield and Stockbridge. Volunteers also helped Rutland residents salvage what they could from flooded homes and cleaned the muck from basements. Here, as elsewhere, the unsung heroes, and there were many hundred working anonymously in all the flood-damaged towns, were the ones who helped people shovel out their basements, heave sodden couches to the street, and haul the mess to dumps and Dumpsters.

In a moving piece published in the Rutland Herald, Sabataso wrote, "Over the years, I've often had doubts about my generation" but "within efforts at Restoring Rutland and I Am Vermont Strong, my generation has been leading the way. While our volunteers' ages have varied widely, the core group of leaders has been largely in their 20s and 30s."

So many of these stories of self-reliance and team spirit were actually happening that they got the attention of the national media. One story oft-repeated involved a phone conversation between Vermont Governor Peter Shumlin and Governor Chris Christie of New Jersey soon after the flood. Christie asked Shumlin how Vermont was doing, and Shumlin answered 'pretty well'. When Christie wondered how that could be, Shumlin retorted, "You have to understand that every Vermonter has a backhoe and a tractor, while in other states you have a Mercedes and a BMW."

This disaster felt different somehow. Everyone was awed by it.

THROUGH THE LENS:
SEEING THE HEART OF VERMONT
Published in the Rutland Herald and Times Argus on Sept. 23, 2011
By JEB WALLACE-BRODEUR

The home sat torn open like a freshly shucked oyster. Two days prior, the raging White River had peeled off two walls and the floor had been bent down to the ground. Sheared-off two-by-fours, which once framed the walls, hung from the red interior like rotting teeth from swollen gums.

An antique piano, now silt-covered, lay overturned in an adjacent room. An ornate Oriental rug was crumpled into a mouldering ball. A delicate porcelain tub was almost comically filled to overflow with compacted mud.

Everywhere lay the artifacts of someone's shattered life: strewn clothing, lamps, books, dishes, furniture. All dripping and muddied by the flood.

Among the ruins of the building, now more of a lean-to than a home, stood that someone: Don Fielder. He surveyed the devastation wearing a loose cotton shirt and khakis, a cup of coffee in his hand.

What do you say to someone who has just lost it all? To arrive here, I had driven down miles of cobbled-together roads, often barely wide enough to keep all four wheels out of small chasms.

When the roads ended, I walked. I came upon this home in Stockbridge, at the confluence of the White River and Lillietown Brook, unannounced and perhaps unwelcome.

Now I was faced with this theater set of disaster. I looked at the bare ruins of Fielder's kitchen and noticed the intricate and colorful mosaic surrounding the windows and doors.

"You had a beautiful home," I said. "That tile work is exquisite." He looked at me and smiled warmly. "Isn't it incredible? I think I may be able to save most of it."

Many people think you need a good eye to be a photographer. For me, it's more important to have an open mind.

Walking into someone's life with a camera is scary. Especially during times of trouble. You never know what may happen. But after almost 20 years of photographing Vermonters, I've learned to trust the goodness of people.

I try to enter every situation without preconception and with genuine curiosity. I can count on one hand the number of negative interactions I've had in my career. I feel fortunate to have interacted with so many decent people over the years. That decency seemed only to amplify during this disaster.

When I walked on to Don Fielder's property, I had no idea what sort of reception I might receive. I was apprehensive, but my curiosity was rewarded with a nugget of humanity that will stay with me. Numerous people since Tropical Storm Irene have asked with great concern how I'm doing.

The assumption is that this must have taken an emotional toll on me. While I was drained by documenting the endless destruction, the generosity and warmth of those affected by the storm was inspiring.

This disaster felt different somehow. Everyone was awed by it. I saw some hugs, but almost no tears. The power of the water seemed to wash away feelings of victimization and despair. People wanted to share their stories. To show their little, personal slices of the communal destructive pie.

Walking through the slop on aptly named Water Street in Northfield, I paused at a large yellow home. The muddy yard was filled with furniture and belongings.

The owner of the building, a rental property, noticed me.

Rebecca Trower shouted over to me, "Hey! You with the newspaper? Come here, I want to show you my house."

We spent the next hour chatting and looking through the gutted remains of her building. Trower didn't dwell on the damage. Mostly she wanted me to know how helpful people had been to her.

She said a group of four high school kids had been there every day, working tirelessly. She didn't even know all their names, but she wanted their efforts to be mentioned in the newspaper.

Volunteers were everywhere. I visited Waterbury almost every day and saw the same crew of Green Mountain Club employees, chased out of the mountains by the storm, completely covered in mud and hefting five-gallon pails of slop out of people's basements.

There were volunteers sitting on the lawn washing mountains of dishes and cutlery in big soapy buckets outside the Wesley United Methodist Church. Anne Imhoff, an elderly resident of Parker Court, had a team of helpers going through her belongings to see what could be salvaged.

"These people are just so wonderful," she said to me.

In Duxbury, a homeowner had lowered a hay bale conveyor through a blown-out hole in his cinder block foundation. Endless pails of muck were riding up the conveyor to be dumped on an impressive pile by a bucket brigade of strong backs.

On Camel's Hump Road, Mike Feulner's home stood perched on an island. Ridley Brook had swept 10 feet of earth away from his foundation and deposited boulders everywhere.

A group of volunteers from the Homeland Security Office in Williston had spent the day removing spoiled drywall and salvaging what could be saved. Surveying his cozy home, now teetering above a rocky moat, Feulner said, "Can you believe these folks are using their vacation time to help me?"

In Rochester, a town that took some creative route finding to get to, citizens gathered in the school gymnasium for a hot lunch and updates on efforts to get them reconnected with the outside world.

Stories were swapped and the atmosphere was upbeat. The shared experience of the storm seemed to have made a close-knit town even tighter. Up the street, by the loading dock at Mac's Market, a group of employees rested on overturned milk crates. The store had been without power since the storm.

Out front, shopping carts full of perishables sat in the parking lot, food free for the taking. "Most of that's only fit for pigs at this point," said a worker. "But we helped a lot of people get some food in their bellies this week."

More than a week after the storm, I got a day off, Labor Day. My wife had been volunteering the past three days in Waterbury. Her legs were bruised from carrying heavy loads.

Amy Molina, athletic director at U-32, sent out a Facebook message that a friend at Weston's Mobile Home Park in Berlin was in need. I left my camera at home and spent the day with my wife and son, and a large crew of familiar faces, in the rain and mud at Weston's.

We saved what we could and discarded a lot more. By the end of the day, huge mounds of people's lives lined the sloppy streets. The refrain of the day from the devastated homeowners was: "Thank you, I don't know what we would have done without you."

Tropical Storm Irene was a historic event. And (hopefully) a once-in-a-lifetime opportunity for a journalist. While the scenes of destruction were heartbreaking and awe-inspiring, the human heart of this little state was never more evident. And it fills me with hope.

By the end of the day,
huge mounds of people's lives
lined the sloppy streets.

Moretown is a good example of Shumlin's observation. Not only was the town organized before the flood with an emergency plan in effect and daily and sometimes twice-daily town meetings to keep everyone informed in the weeks after Irene, but it seemed that everyone in town was capable of doing tasks that city people might be clueless about. Meriden Nelson's home was flooded four to six feet deep on the first floor but the 71-year-old was out on Monday morning with one of the town vehicles, plowing up mud and sediment from Main Street. The foundation on his home had been undermined and possessions on the first floor were covered in mud. Neighbors by the dozens volunteered to help him.

"It happened spontaneously," Selectman Clark Amadon recalled. Both bridges on Route 100B had been affected and the town school was flooded. Quickly, residents erected tents and organized field trips so the children could attend some form of class. While the town thought the school clean-up might take a week or so, it turned out to be much more time-consuming as, after the schoolhouse was disinfected, officials discovered asbestos in the building, which then had to be removed, prompting a second clean-up effort. It was three weeks before the building could be used.

With so many basements and first floors needing to be cleared out, residents developed methods for doing so efficiently through practice.

"There was a constant traipsing back and forth with Kubota tractors, picking up debris from homes, taking it to roll-off Dumpsters, hour after hour, volunteers working till 9:30, 10 o'clock at night, then returning at 7 in the morning," Amadon recalled.

Liz Harris, a mother of five who has lived in Moretown all her life, rode her bike through town each day, several trips most days, checking in with people to see what they needed, getting it and delivering it, along with messages and information. Michelle Beard and her husband Kevin took it upon themselves to make sure everyone got fed. Michelle normally worked in Waterbury and was temporarily out of work due to flood damage. The Beards organized a kind of hot breakfast, lunch and dinner operation with food donated from local restaurants.

At the point when the work seemed endless, resident Bobby Mays took his kids to Maine for a quick reprieve, and came home with 150 pounds of lobster and clams as well. It was raining the day they fashioned an old-fashioned clam and lobster bake complete with local corn on the cob, but no one seemed to notice as local musicians played and residents enjoyed a reprieve from the drudgery.

"We were at the town hall the day after the storm, people eating with tears rolling down their faces and then we wiped the tears and got to work," town clerk Lamson said. "You look at life differently now; Irene put it all in perspective. We're appreciative of what we have. My camper was broken into two weeks after the flood, badly vandalized. My aunt asked me how I was taking it so well. I said, 'After what I just saw, after Irene, this is nothing.'"

We were at the town hall the day after the storm, people eating with tears rolling down their faces and then we wiped the tears and got to work.

THE NEW MORETOWN ELEMENTARY: FLOODED SCHOOL MOVES INTO TENT

Published in the Rutland Herald and Times Argus on Sept. 14, 2011

By STEFAN HARD

"Pitching in" gained new meaning Tuesday at Moretown Elementary School, where staff and volunteers erected tents to house students attending the first day of classes on school grounds. Tropical Storm Irene damaged the elementary school building, but not the spirit of this community. Eager to get students back to familiar school grounds, school officials opted for canvas classrooms over bricks and mortar.

Not surprisingly, the school's principal office was in a pop-up camper. It was operating in the school parking lot, within sight of the tiny tent city that has sprung up in the school's ballfield.

The school nurse's office was set up in a tent with a desk and two Army-style cots. Another tent housed the school's special-education office equipped with a desk and two laptops. Electrical extension cords ran to the camper and tents to provide power.

The white-clad and green-roofed Moretown Elementary School building remains off limits due to contamination from floodwaters that inundated the school in August's flash flooding on the nearby Mad River. The torrential rains that produced the destructive floodwaters came from Tropical Storm Irene, which hit Vermont hard, destroying roadways, isolating towns and destroying homes, businesses and infrastructure.

Across the state, flooded-out communities have responded with creativity, hard work and Yankee know-how. The "new" Moretown Elementary School was a prime example of that enduring spirit.

On Tuesday, the students seemed happy and comfortable inside their spacious classroom tents, where a full roster of teachers engaged them in the full range of subjects, albeit with some tweaks in the schedule to allow students time to stretch outside the temporary white canvas enclosures. Conveniently, the weather was warm and breezy, and daylight meant no need for artificial lighting.

Last week, the pre-K-through-12 school started classes for three days by sending students on field trips as the school building was cleaned and repaired.

Administrators had hoped to have students back inside Monday, but the building failed a test for bacteria levels and had to be decontaminated for a second time. That meant students went on a fourth field trip Monday -- this time to the Echo Lake Aquarium and Science Center in Burlington.

On Tuesday, that changed when the school grounds opened for classes.

Principal Duane Pierson, dressed in shorts and a bright red T-shirt, took calls Tuesday inside his cozy pop-up camper as administrative assistant Pam Kathan worked on the other side of the camper with a laptop and printer.

Pierson said the unwelcomed news delivered Saturday that the school building was still contaminated was followed by a frantic, 24-hour period of logistics work, as planning took place for improvised outdoor classes.

Word went out quickly through a list of parents' email addresses and the online Front Page Forum about the range of items that would be necessary to pull off the outdoor school. Thanks to generous community support and response, nearly everything needed materialized by Monday evening, including generators for the tent classrooms, coolers, camp chairs, pads, special busing, and breakfast and lunch.

Among the contributors Pierson listed were Ben & Jerry's Homemade, Sugarbush Resort and Bongiorno's Italian Resta for food items; First Student for busing; and Valley Rent All for tents and generators.

Student Colin Green, 11, even brought his own chair for classes Tuesday. It was made out of half a cardboard box strengthened by black duct tape.

A call for presenters to entertain and educate the Moretown students also was sent out, and the reaction was extraordinary, officials said. School librarian Meg Allison said she had received so many offers of help that she had to turn some away.

One of the presenters Tuesday was Warren science educator Bob Lisaius, also known as Dinoman, who taught children about a massive meteorite that was believed to have caused the extinction of the dinosaurs.

"We have just seen overwhelming generosity from the community," Pierson said. "The kids have been awesome. They're excited to be here. The teachers have been phenomenal - I can't say enough about them."

Pre-K students were hosted by Precious Moments School in Moretown on Tuesday.

Pierson said he is hopeful that the school will pass its next environmental test, clearing Moretown Elementary School for normal operations by week's end.

*"Pitching in" gained
new meaning*

Likewise, in Northfield along the Dog River where the Wall-Goldfinger Complex had been swamped by floodwaters, 20 friends and families showed up to help clean Rocky's Repair Shop. When that was done, Rockland Sanders got on his tractor to help his neighbors.

Official help was well coordinated as well. By late Sunday, the Red Cross had opened 11 shelters – in Barre, Bennington, Brattleboro, Bristol, Enosburg, Hartford, Middlebury, Rutland, St. Albans, St. Johnsbury and Springfield. Volunteers came in from all around the country to man these centers. In Plymouth, between the Red Cross and the astonishing number of volunteers who showed up in the first few days after the storm, coordinators had created a stream-lined process to help residents get food and supplies, fill out FEMA forms and find shelter where necessary. Indeed, so many volunteers showed up that a notebook was quickly filled with the names of people from Mississippi to Maine offering their services.

The Salvation Army opened a disaster recovery center in Rutland and a canteen center in Ludlow, feeding hundreds, distributing clean-up kits widely, and offering appliances to affected homeowners after the storm.

It didn't take long for the Vermont National Guard to get organized either. By Tuesday, relief supplies had arrived at Vermont's National Guard headquarters in a convoy of 30 trucks and FEMA had flown in food, water and other necessities to residents of Cavendish, Granville, Hancock, Killington, Mendon, Marlboro, Pittsfield, Plymouth, Rochester, Stockbridge, Strafford, Stratton and Wardsboro. Throughout the state, reconstruction and rescue efforts were aided by National Guard troops from Maine, Virginia, West Virginia, South Carolina and Illinois.

In Waterbury, the Vermont National Guard was essential in the effort to safely evacuate patients from the Vermont State Hospital the night of the storm; other troops helped evacuate people and monitor dangerous roads in Westminster, Berlin, Dover, Randolph and Berlin. During the early stages of the operation, two guard vehicles were overcome by water, but the soldiers later escaped unharmed.

Blackhawk helicopters on loan from Illinois to the Vermont Air Guard (the Guard's own helicopters were deployed in Iraq) not only transported emergency food, water and other supplies to dozens of stranded

Norwich cadet, Ben Caroll, helps remove mud from a destroyed home on Union Street in Northfield.

Brian Halligan of Pittsfield stands before his wrecked home, which he left a half hour before it collapsed.

communities from the base in South Burlington but they transported FEMA Administrator Craig Fugate along with Governor Peter Shumlin, Senator Patrick Leahy, D-VT, Senator Bernie Sanders, I-VT, and Representative Peter Welch, D-VT, in to inaccessible areas so they could assess the damage. In all, 249 Vermont National Guard soldiers worked on the rescue and reconstruction effort. In Jamaica alone, emergency coordinator Paul Fraser says their work was essential in the effort to rebuild Pikes Falls Road.

Guard units from Vermont and six other states were also instrumental in the monumental feat of rebuilding Route 131 where the 200-yard section known as the Cavendish Canyon had stranded residents. When enough work was done for the AOT and its contractors to take over and the troops had returned home, Cavendish Town Manager Rich Strong told them at a thank-you celebration, "We've grown to know you and love you and what you've done for our community."

In Stockbridge, Army National Guard soldiers from Virginia, West Virginia, South Carolina and Maine worked with the Vermont Agency of Transportation and local contractors on the formidable task of rebuilding Route 107, which had been annihilated by floodwaters. Maine National Guard soldiers stabilized the road so the rebuilding process could begin.

Unfortunately, another death occurred among the Vermont National Guard troops working on Vermont roads. Master Sgt. Shawn Stocker was thought to have suffered a heart attack on the way from the Proctorsville Fire Station to a road project in Cavendish.

Stocker, 46, was a state corrections officer from West Rutland who had served with the Guard in Iraq; he just returned from an overseas deployment a few weeks before Irene. FEMA does not list his death as flood-related so he is not included in the official list of those who died during or as a result of Tropical Storm Irene.

However, two other Vermonters who died after the storm are listed as Irene-related fatalities. One was Anthony Doleszny of Brattleboro who apparently rode a bicycle around barricades on Williams Street and fell into the Whetstone Brook a few days after the storm. A Woodstock man also died when he fell downstairs while cleaning up after Irene; the name was not released.

We've grown to know you and love you and what you've done for our community.

MISSION LAST MINUTE GUARD SEND-OFF ACCOMPLISHED

Published in the Rutland Herald and Times Argus on Oct. 1, 2011
By CRISTINA KUMKA

The school was just the down the road.

For Karen Pezzetti, it wouldn't be that easy.

The last of the National Guard members who helped repair this state's roads and its residents' spirit after Tropical Storm Irene were leaving at 7 a.m. Friday on the dot — an hour earlier than when students had to be there.

She said the higher-ups in the Army wouldn't cut her a break and leave later so the kids could wave goodbye from the front lawn of the small, rural school.

They had orders.

She was thinking about how she could make her own.

Pezzetti, a dedicated volunteer at the center serving meals to the troops for weeks as well as a special education teacher and emergency coordinator at the school, knew she wanted to send the last remaining 13 Maine National Guard members off in style but didn't know how she would do it.

They were here the longest and she got to know them personally. They had nicknames like Shirley, Chihuahua and Chucka. They had families back home, marriages, babies — just like she did. They chatted and ate breakfast together. One night they even danced.

As she sat with the troops at their last meal at the Armed Forces Reserve Center on Post Road Thursday night, she started her own mission to show how appreciative she was of theirs.

The eyes of her husband, David, started rolling.

Master Sgt. Kevin Walsh said it was akin to a "logistical nightmare."

Other volunteers cheered her on.

She called the school's jazz band director, other teachers and then Rutland Town School Principal Pati Beaumont.

How would they get kids to line up that early with flags and signs to say thanks?

Beaumont offered to do an AlertNow — an automated phone message sent to all parents typically reserved for snow days.

It worked. At 6:50 a.m. Friday morning, the cars of parents started pulling up in the CVPS parking lot. Kids hopped out like they hadn't missed a wink of sleep, gripped flags and banners.

They stood, hardly in formation, on the sidewalk directly across the street from the sign that announced what that big building on the hill was and what those camouflaged trucks were doing there.

Good. The troops couldn't possibly miss them now, Karen thought.

"It's amazing how wonderful they were being here helping us," said Alicia Robideau, 13, a member of the school's jazz band who held up the sign she made the night before, after getting the message from the principal.

Eight-year-old Gianna Pezzetti, Karen's daughter, held as much as she could fit in her hands that morning — a flag and a banner.

She wore red. Her mom picked out the outfit for her, she said.

What did she do when mom and dad were volunteering all that time?

Gianna hung out with friends. But now, she was there to thank the soldiers.

In one excited burst, she ripped open her red fleece zip-up and proudly showed off her shirt. It had a big green outline of Vermont on it and read, "Coming Together in the Green Mountains."

In one hour's time, on a random Thursday night, Pezzetti and the school made it happen.

The kids joined more than a hundred others — even Gov. Peter Shumlin in thanking about 300 troops from at least five states for their work here. They wrote signs, waved, made calls or just shook hands in appreciation.

When the trucks, trailers and one Hummer drove past the kids, they cheered — both the kids and the soldiers.

Some of the kids were disappointed there weren't more troops or big trucks to look at.

But they weren't the only ones who wanted to see.

Christ the King students lined up on Main Street in Rutland the day before, to wave thanks to the Virginia Guard members, too.

"They brought a sense of community back to us. This whole storm brought our Rutland community closer together. Even when we were serving dinner and stuff, there was a whole sense of working together and sharing things together," Karen Pezzetti said. Beaumont said the gathering was for a good cause and a good lesson.

"From a civic standpoint, people talk about how we don't teach our kids civics. Sometimes, living civically is better learning," she said.

One of the most formidable road reconstruction challenges involved Route 107. Tropical Storm Irene's rain had caused the White River to rise several feet above flood stage, sweeping away bridges and embankments and annihilating 107. The West Virginia Guard's 20-ton dump trucks had hauled 450 tons of dirt and rock a day along Stockbridge sections of the road for several weeks, establishing a roadbed so that local contractors working with the Vermont Agency of Transportation could try to rebuild the road before winter. At least 10 miles of 107 were simply gone.

Doug Casella of Casella Construction, headquartered in Rutland, and his crew took on the job working with Frank W. Whitcomb Construction Co. of Colchester. There was no way to get enough building material into Route 107 from the Bethel end of the road, so an ingenious method was devised. Whitcomb quarried thousands of tons of 500 million-year-old rocks called Monkton quartzite and then hauled it by truck to Burlington where it was loaded into specialized train cars, then brought to Bethel where Casella's crew used it to rebuild the road.

REBUILDING ROUTE 107 WITH ANCIENT ROCKS AND BIG TRUCKS
Published in the Rutland Herald and Times Argus on Nov. 2, 2011
By YVONNE DALEY

In the months since Tropical Storm Irene literally inundated roughly 10 miles of Route 107 through Stockbridge and Bethel, Doug Casella and his team of men have been reconstructing the road from scratch with their giant trucks, excavators and backhoes. It's been a formidable task. Route 107, a narrow passage hugging the White River, is a major east-west link between Interstate 89, Killington and western Vermont, and the flood not only took out the road but dug deep into the roadbed and sidebanks.

Already, 35,000 tons of Monkton quartzite, a very durable, red or pink-tinted rock over 500 million years old, has been used to build up the roadbed.

Just getting the rocks to the 38 washouts along 107 has required quite a bit of ingenuity.

The rocks are quarried at the F.W. Whitcomb Construction quarry in Colchester, hauled by truck to the rail yard in Burlington, then transported 76 miles to Bethel. At the Bethel rail yard, railcars are tipped sideways and one side is lowered, allowing the rock to be dumped down an embankment where backhoes deposit them into giant Euclid trucks, their wheels alone 10 feet tall.

Because the trucks are so heavy, they cannot cross the bridge onto Route 107 but instead are driven right into the White River, which is flowing quite briskly due to recent rains. The Euclid drivers then deposit the rocks along the river where backhoes are used to set the rocks in place.

F.W. Whitcomb president Frank "Chip" Whitcomb said everyone is getting pretty efficient at the operation - the workers were able to unload 21 railroad cars of rock in 17 minutes one day this week. At 90 tons a carload, that's nearly 2,000 tons of rock.

Whitcomb is also trucking rocks down Interstate 89, but permission to use the Interstate runs out next week.

The rock is exceptionally durable. State geologist Laurence Becker said Monkton quartzite is "an interesting rock," that was deposited in what was an extensive but shallow sea and then a sandy beach in the Burlington area 500 million years ago. The quarry where he is working is quite deep and shows ripple marks in the rock from when the sand turned into sandstone and, eventually under pressure, became quartzite.

Whitcomb and Casella acknowledge they are working against time and weather as they strive to get the road built before winter. "Realistically, we need to have decent weather in November," Whitcomb conceded.

For example, Casella points out that the base road the workers are using is substantially lower than Route 107 was before the flood. It will need to be raised significantly to prevent future flooding. Additionally, silt islands have built up in the White River, leading Casella to express concern about future flooding.

"Anyone who thinks you can keep a river from going where it wants to go is dreaming," he said.

Casella Construction is one of several local firms that have found themselves working long hours in Vermont since Irene. Doug Casella founded Casella Construction in 1975 fresh from graduating from Mount St. Joseph Academy. It's rare that he spends as much time as he has this fall in Vermont, as most of his jobs take him out of state where, he said, the work has been more demolition than reconstruction. His crews went to help after Hurricane Katrina.

"It's the first time I've been in Rutland for three weeks in a row in 20 years," he said.

Earlier this fall, Casella Construction helped in the reconstruction of Route 4, bringing well over 100,000 yards of material to create a base and stabilize the slopes on either side of the washed out road through Mendon.

While what they've done is impressive, Casella said it's not as impressive as what Irene did. "What we're able to do (in Mendon) in 15 to 18 days, she did in 10 hours and we had 40 or 50 men on that job," he says.

Casella has been struck by the difference in attitude between Vermonters and residents of other parts of the country where he's responded to disasters. Here, he says, no one's waiting around to be rescued or complaining about the inconvenience. People with the means to help are stepping forward.

And he's also been pleased to work hand and hand with his competitors - the Belden Company and Markowski Construction, along with Mosher Excavating.

"What was pretty cool, we all had our kids working with us," he said. "I don't think in another state, they would have worked together like that."

That aside, Casella says the work has not only been daunting, but heartbreaking. One of his crewmembers lost his house and the men are working in "our backyards, our state, our communities, seeing what happened to our friends. That's been sobering."

Anyone who thinks they can keep a river from going where it wants to go, is dreaming.

Meanwhile, Vermont Agency of Transportation officials were busy reconstructing roads from Wilmington to Smugglers Notch, an enterprise that required the hiring of thousands of outside contractors and a coordination effort beyond anyone's experience.

With more than 50 state roads dismantled and 250 road closures, the state opened incident command centers in Rutland and Dummerston, and in three days had carved out exit routes for all 13 towns that had previously been isolated. Over the course of the next few months, the agency not only oversaw the rebuilding of dismantled state roads and acquisition of the equipment and materials to do so but also coordination between state and federal officials and private contractors along with the complex documentation required so contractors could be paid and Vermont could be reimbursed by FEMA.

On top of that, with so many state employees relocated to the incident command centers, the state AOT had to make arrangements for them to be housed and fed. It was efficiency on the fly with dozens of people taking on jobs they had never done before and working with people who came to the command centers as strangers and left as friends. Within the first month alone, three programmers, Ben Lind, Justin Hadley and Reid Kinirey created a system for recording and tracking the complex data, photographs and progress reports needed to document work on 390 construction sites that fell under the purview of the AOT's Rutland Region Incident Command Center after the storm. Their computer system is expected to be a model for future emergencies.

Hard as it was, impossible as it had seemed on August 29, the job got done. By early November, Route 107 was the last state road still only partially open.

TRACKING THE RESPONSE: AOT PROGRAMMERS CREATE SYSTEM TO TRACK FUTURE DISASTERS
Published in the Rutland Herald and Times Argus on Oct. 31, 2011
By YVONNE DALEY

A computerized system developed by three men working at the Agency of Transportation's regional center after Tropical Storm Irene may well serve as a model for managing future emergencies. Three programmers, Ben Lind, Justin Hadley and Reid Kiniry, created a system for recording and tracking the complex data, photographs and progress reports needed to document work on 390 construction sites that fell under the purview of the AOT's Rutland Region Incident Command Center after the storm.

And they did it in three weeks' time.

"They created something well above what was asked of them, something that can be used in future disasters. It came right out of their brains," says Chris Williams of Moretown, the planning section chief at the Rutland Region ICC.

Gil Newbury, who headed the command center, explains how overwhelming the task appeared to be - with more than 700 sites in roughly 75 towns identified as needing some sort of action after floodwaters tore through Vermont.

He described the system Lind, Kinirey and Handley created as including "a kind of electronic shoebox" to hold the more than 10,000 before, during and after photographs of each construction site; these in turn were linked digitally to all the necessary data for each site, such as federal and state estimates of cost, the real cost data and other pertinent information.

Essentially, the system allows AOT personnel to click onto an interactive map and view all the data and images for each individual project. It's a massive amount of information; photos alone take up 437 gigabytes of space.

Newbury says simply, "It was brilliant."

Williams is normally a state bridge engineer. After 28 years with the AOT, he found it refreshing "to see actual progress. I get restless at the pace sometimes. We had a real sense of accomplishment here."

Tropical Storm Irene had a head start on the AOT employees, arriving on Aug. 28, a Sunday. By Wednesday, people from all over the state, not just from the Agency of Transportation's various offices, but, as Newbury puts it, "every unemployed college student east of the Mississippi to old veterans of building roads" were coming together to create something he described as "invigorating and stunning."

Their task was to not only coordinate and document the state's efforts in rebuilding state roads from Bennington to Leicester but also coordinate the voluminous paperwork required to ensure that dozens of hired contractors and their crews got paid and each contract was properly documented under federal reimbursement requirements.

The second part of the job - coordinating hundreds of bids, contracts and payment records - fell to Morgan Tyminski of Rutland, who took on the role of administrative section chief during the emergency.

Working with a team of about 10, Tyminski developed both a paper and a computer model for identifying and assessing needs, tracking each problem area, awarding bids, overseeing contracts, verifying work and sending the necessary paperwork to Montpelier.

All this began at the AOT regional office on McKinley Avenue in Rutland, an office normally staffed by less than 10 people. Tyminski, who normally works as the Rutland District 3 administrative assistant, described the first two weeks as both hectic and fulfilling with 80 or more people using the Rutland office, working elbow to elbow, in corners and under desks until the state leased the former Peace of Mind building on Route 4 in Mendon for the ICC team.

After weeks of working cheek by jowl, however, the various team members had bonded so well that they set up their new working spaces close to one another. Newbury, who is customarily the dean of the AOT's internal training center and its lead teacher, christened the new headquarters The Hotel California, alluding to the Eagles' song with the line, "You can check out any time you like but you can never leave."

From all appearances, no one was doing much checking out, but rather put in 12 to 15 hour days, sometimes seven days a week, so much so that Newbury would have to send people home or even drive them home because he thought they were too tired to drive. In two months, he only went home to St. Albans three times.

While this might sound like drudgery, the rock music blasting from the wrap-around sound system, the bowls of candy hither and yon, the foam dart guns ready for firing and the stories of shared meals give evidence that this was a team that not only worked well together, but also played well together.

That was evident at Newbury's station, surrounded by jail bars made from black crepe paper, hung for his 50th birthday, and the poster behind his desk that shows him with his dog and his age in dog years.

Newbury's father died during the emergency response effort, on Sept. 22, and one of his father's favorite sayings graced the center's wall, "Life is a story. Live a story worth telling." That was the message Newbury imparted day after day as his team tackled the work. His tie with its reproductions of a World War II cartoon by Bill Mauldin underlined that message. On it, infantrymen Willie is saying to Joe, "Yesterday you saved my life and today I'm going to pay you back. Here's my last pair of dry socks."

Newbury's enthusiasm, even as the team closed the emergency office last week, was also apparent in the way he extolled the gifts and contributions of each employee, deflecting praise and credit their way.

For example, no sooner had Williams praised his team's efforts and Newbury's leadership than Newbury spread the praise around. "Chris had the vision," he said. "He saw the tsunami of information coming and he responded."

Tsunami, indeed. Equipment had to be found. Hotel rooms for the state workers had to be found. Food for the workers had to be supplied. Tom Trahant, whom Newbury describes as "the elder statesman," had the job of communicating with the outside world, meaning not only to the public and within state agencies, but also between the various National Guard regiments, American Red Cross and federal officials.

Anne Candon, who grew up in Pittsford but now works in Montpelier, came to the ICC to help organize the effort. "Whether you needed a bulldozer or a bagel, Ann's group found out where to get it and how to pay for it," Newbury said.

Then there was Chris Taft, a young gun of 27 whose job working for a construction company was winding down when Irene struck. He joined the ICC team and found himself ordering millions of dollars worth of materials. His synopsis of the past two months' work: "It's been fun."

Judy Gilmour of Tinmouth develops contracts for work on state highway at the Rutland district office, a process that normally takes four months. At the ICC, she was cranking them out in five days.

And Ann Gammell from Barre found herself functioning like an executive engineer at the ICC, from tracking down bulldozers and excavators and organizing state crews to coordinating with the National Guard. Of

Todd Keehan and Josiane Deletine's yard and home before Tropical Storm Irene and after.

the 15-hour days she put it, she says blithely, "It was a madhouse but it was fun."

"That's what I mean," says Newbury. "My hardest job is getting people to understand the magnitude of what they did."

State officials certainly recognized the importance of their work.

"The Rutland ICC did not just play a critical role in helping to restore Vermont's transportation infrastructure, it is the very reason all state roads in southwest Vermont were reopened just six weeks following such a devastating storm," Secretary of Transportation Brian Searles said last week.

As for the future, Newbury says big questions need to be answered. Transportation crews reconstructed roads and put streams back where they were, but he doubts that is the end of it. Deeper, more complex questions need to be asked - Are our state roads in the right places? Should the rivers be allowed to be where they insist on flowing or where we want them to go? Are there roads that shouldn't be rebuilt at all?

"What vision is going to come from Irene?" he asks. "Maybe we need to heal the rivers. Gravity always wins in the end. Irene is nothing more than a study in gravity."

Central Vermont Public Service, which at one point had a shattered distribution system with several substations out, lines down, utility poles smashed to smithereens and 73,000 customers without service, restored service to almost all customers in a week, an effort company officials had first predicted would take several weeks. To do so, employees built entirely new transmission lines in areas where there were no roads, many working 18 to 20-hour shifts. In the first few days when there was no access to places like Stratton, Jamaica and Rochester, employees rode off-road motorcycles and dirt bikes to check on lines, slept in their cars or at their desks. Deb Weaver, a customer care advocate who helped field some of the 19,000 calls the company received on August 28, the first day of the storm, found herself "shar(ing) a lot of tears with customers … They just needed someone to talk to, and we were able to provide that to them."

Still and all, while resiliency and cooperation were on full display throughout Vermont, the months ahead presented huge dilemmas, particularly for communities like Wilmington, Waterbury and Brandon whose downtowns were so badly impacted. Throughout the fall and early winter all three communities were having public meetings to strategize ways to move ahead and attendance remained high. While some residents of these towns were downhearted, for the most part the atmosphere was positive and forward-looking.

The town of Dover, a neighbor of Wilmington, provided both money and expertise to its neighbor in hopes of salvaging the historic downtown and Wilmington officials organized several efforts to help businesses remain downtown. Waterbury established a non-profit organization called Rebuild Waterbury to organize volunteers and raise funds for recovery efforts as well as find housing for those made homeless by Irene. And in Brandon, town officials were exploring the Vermont Downtown Program as one of many efforts to revitalize their ravaged downtown. Months and years of work, refinancing and rebuilding lay ahead but as evidenced by a public meeting in Brandon in mid-November, determination to work together remained strong. As Bernie Carr, owner of Carr's Florist, put it, "Don't be scared to get involved."

You Can Get There From Here

Ben Bemis likes to ride his motorcycle. He hadn't slept at all Sunday night, thinking about the tropical storm that had dropped its heavy burden on Vermont all day. He knew the roads were bad. No one knew how bad. Bemis threw his motorbike in the back of his truck and drove from his home in Thetford to the Central Vermont Public Service office in Royalton and jumped on the motorcycle. Bemis, 56, is the Royalton operations manager for CVPS.

Over the next day, he forged his way on snowmobile trails and along blown out roads, traversing 93 miles through towns that had sections that looked as if they had been bombed, from Stockbridge, to Gaysville to Rochester and back again, all the while observing the condition of poles and wires, substations and transmission machinery.

Meanwhile, Duane Dickinson, 49, of West Rutland, had an idea about how to get into the backside of Jamaica where the West Jamaica and Pikes Falls Road had been chopped up into something that once resembled roads but now looked more like rushing river, rubble piles, boulder dams and shattered asphalt. It could be weeks, maybe months, before the roads would be rebuilt. How could they restore electric lines if the CVSP workers couldn't get to them?

Dickinson, a forestry manager with CVPS, "confiscated" a co-workers' kid's mountain bike and rode into Jamaica through Stratton, like Bemis finding few intact roads and making his way through woods, along VAST trails and through chasms, at times wading through chest-high water carrying the bike. Meter readers Tim Madore and Charlie Daigneault were also navigating this ravaged terrain on mountain bikes, cataloguing the damage in Wardsboro, West Jamaica and East Dover.

These men were not alone. While utility workers often encounter situations that require strength and endurance, the resourcefulness of these workers is worth noting, as well as the dangers they faced.

Indeed, "a tree crew working on Hogback mountain got trapped after washouts and high water cut off all escape routes," Steve Costello, director of public affairs, wrote in a company publication about Tropical Storm Irene. Additionally, a utility worker and meter reader were stranded in Shrewsbury when roads got washed out and two Brattleboro area workers had to spend the night with customers after high water prevented them from traveling.

Bemis and Dickinson's stories show how challenging just assessing the damage could be.

Bemis was trying to get to a transmission power line in Stockbridge but every way there had been rearranged by the White River. He was "dumbfounded. There was no edge, no road, as far as I could see," he said. He tried various trails and eventually made his way to Old Mount Hunger Road between Barnard and Stockbridge, but trees blocked the road. He ran into some people who were trying to walk out from their demolished homes and they helped him lift his bike over the trees.

Eventually, he came to Fort Defiance Road off Route 12. It was all washed out but he was able to work his way through the ditches back to Old Mount Hunger Road, where he got cell service and was able to operate a mechanical airbrake that needed to be switched before further work on the power lines could be done.

As he tried various routes to Rochester, Bemis ran into people who suggested ways to circumnavigate washouts. At one point, a stranger loaned him tools so he could work on his bike. When he finally made his way to the Gaysville Bridge, they'd already heard of him.

From there, he rode to the Rochester substation. It had been destroyed – that was the word Bemis used. Destroyed. A little doe was wrapped around one of the utility poles, drowned. When he got into town, a local contractor named Ray Harvey was cleaning out a culvert; he loaned Bemis gas so he could get home.

While he was called a superhero, Bemis says, "I was just gathering information." A week or so after the storm when Bemis was "on a fun run," he had an accident, knocked himself out, broke his collarbone and four ribs. He's recuperating fine.

In Jamaica, Dickinson, Daigneault and Madore pedaled miles of back roads, hiking trails and carried their bikes through rivers and mud to find out what CVPS had left in Wardsboro, Jamaica and Dover. Dickinson tried riding up the West Jamaica Road but it was pretty washed out so he carried the bike through the woods to where he could climb over blow-downs to the other side of the river. That meant wading through the river, carrying the bike, using a combination of climbing, wading and pedaling to get as far as he could. He did much the same along Pikes Falls Road, or at least until "there was just a canyon and I couldn't go any further."

Dickinson carried a notebook stuffed in his back, recording what poles were on the ground; he got to a place where everything was gone – poles and ground alike – but the lines were still intact, suspended from two poles remaining where more used to be. Later, he found a new trail along Pikes Falls Road but it ended with a "40 or 50-foot drop mountainside to mountainside, so steep I couldn't traverse."

Like Bemis, Dickinson eventually found a way, in his case an old bulldozed logging road that he took to Old Stage Coach Road, finally making his way to Wardsboro by yet another road. Eventually, he found two different ways to get in to these parts of Jamaica. These routes allowed CVPS to install poles and string transmission lines long before the roads were built by bringing material and workers in by an ingenious use of back-road vehicles.

"Cycling is not a difficult task for me," Dickinson said. He averages 3,000 to 4,000 miles on the road a year.

CVPS had restored power to the approximately 70,000 outages statewide by the end of the week.

Lessons Learned, Questions Remain

Alan K. Betts, an atmospheric researcher and meteorologist wrote recently, "More frequent heavy rainfall events are likely, so let us ask the hard questions and plan ahead. Clearly we must leave more room for floodwaters. What was most critical in responding to this crisis? Did we have adequate back-up power systems, food and water supplies and fuel for heavy equipment? Do we need east-west paths across the mountains for emergency use?"

That mix of questions that have a clear yes or no answer with those that do not accurately sums up the scope of question and reflection, discussion and deciding that will follow Irene. On one thing, many will agree: the more prepared we are in the future, the safer we will be. Vermonters were almost unanimously caught off guard.

Steve Costello, spokesperson for CVPS, says the key to the success of its efforts to restore power was preparedness. Days before Tropical Storm Irene's arrival in Vermont, the company had lined up additional crews from Missouri, Kansas, Texas and Illinois. At peak, the company had about 700 outside line, utility and tree workers on site to help with the restoration. Utilities that had experienced less impact from the storm, including Burlington Electric, Green Mountain Power and smaller operations from Ludlow and Lyndonville, offered their assistance. The company had reduced water levels at its generation facilities days before the storm's arrival, surely preventing flooding downstream. Behind the scenes, a veritable cadre of employees well-versed in coordinating disasters of lesser magnitude worked to coordinate the contract and company workers, keep vehicles operating and ensure supplies were delivered to where they would be needed. The company coordinated with Retired Vermont Army National Guard Brigadier General Matt McCoy, CVPS's training coordinator, to feed and house the hundreds of CVPS staff and contract workers.

In Lincoln, residents had taken flood precautions after a terrible flood in 1998. For example, Burnham Hall, a 1920s building near the New Haven River, the culprit in the 98 flood, had been flood-proofed, its lower level fitted with mold-resistant walls and a concrete floor. As warnings of Tropical Storm Irene were broadcasted, volunteers erected temporary flood walls around the building's windows and doors. The river did flood the building but built-in valves worked and the hall was dry in two days.

Likewise, in Barre, good planning and learning from the spring floods probably kept the town from having serious problems in Irene. City Manager Steve Mackenzie said the decision to locate excavators at key locations paid off. One was used to construct a wall of concrete blocks that kept runoff from infiltrating several homes while another was used to open up a culvert that was being overwhelmed by the Potash Brook.

These are lessons for the state of Vermont, which in the coming months will have to face tough decisions and evaluate its own performance. Due to flooding at its quarters in Waterbury, Vermont's Emergency Management Administration was forced to evacuate and relocate as did many other state agencies. As a result, VEMA and the AOT found themselves several days out before they could take action. Now the future of the State Office Complex in Waterbury remains uncertain. Officials estimate a cost of up to $20 million just for clean-up and stabilization efforts of the complex.

Would it be wiser to distribute state offices statewide, centralize them in a few ideal locations or restore the complex, which was quite vital to the economic health of Waterbury and surrounding communities? The Vermont legislature, a special task force and Shumlin's administration will be tackling the issue in 2012 but regardless the outcome of these deliberations, the solution will be complicated and costly.

TWO BROTHERS GO TO BAT FOR VERMONTERS

Published in the Rutland Herald and Times Argus on Nov. 14, 2011

By ANNA GREARSON

Red Sox red, Yankees blue and Pirates black and yellow. Not often do these colors mix well on the baseball diamond, but Saturday evening they blended to make green in support of Vermont farmers impacted by Tropical Storm Irene.

Vermont native Buster Olney, now a reporter covering Major League Baseball with ESPN, joined forces with his brother, Sam Lincoln, a farmer in their hometown of Randolph Center, and hosted the Going to Bat for Vermont Farmers fundraiser at Vermont Technical College starring three upper-echelon baseball executives: New York Yankees general manager Brian Cashman, Pittsburgh Pirates general manager Neal Huntington and former Red Sox GM and current Chicago Cubs president of baseball operations Theo Epstein.

Joining them was Red Sox scout Galen Carr, who lives in Chittenden County. Baseball writer Peter Gammons was slated to attend but was unable to because of a family commitment.

Lincoln, who owns the Lincoln Farm in Randolph Center, was spared Irene's wrath but wanted to do what he could to help the 463 farms covering 10,000 acres affected by Irene.

"Anybody who's lived in Vermont has grown up with the history of the '27 Flood, the '38 Hurricane," Lincoln said. "My own family's farm has a lot of history with the hurricane. These huge weather events happen.

"I know farmers that had their stored crops flooded, their crops in the field flooded, they just got hit hard. They got it from every angle, every bit of the farm flooded. Both Buster and I are feeling very happy we can say, 'Hey, we have this resource, so let's generate some money to help out.'"

Olney had posted pictures of the damage online, which caught the attention of Major League Baseball. Todd Radom, who designs logos for MLB, designed the Going to Bat for Vermont Farmers logo and came up with the slogan itself.

"It's incredible to me - Sam Down on the Farm - to have these celebrities pitching in for a great cause," Lincoln said. "It's a great feeling of gratitude to make a difference to some of these farmers."

Before Saturday's event, which included media availability, a VIP meet-and-greet and dinner with the famous baseball figures, a roundtable discussion about baseball and a raffle, Lincoln estimated ticket sales in the mid-600s and a total of $126,000 raised so far in an online auction, donations and ticket sales.

With a near capacity crowd, that number has undoubtedly multiplied overnight.

"It's almost complete profit, almost everyone has donated - from the cocktails to the food for the meals," Lincoln said. "As soon as I put out the word to my farm friends, people said, 'Hey, I've got cheese, I've got tenderloin, I've got prime rib, and my buddy's got a band.' It's been a great feeling."

"When somebody needs something, Vermonters don't wait around for FEMA. Vermonters are resilient, and they're going to get it done themselves," he continued. "Neighbor helping neighbor. Any division or partisanship between neighbor has melted away and people are helping out in any way they can."

Even if those neighbors are some of the most talked-about figures in sports.

"Vermont loves New Yorkers coming up to ski," said Cashman, who went to college with former UVM men's basketball coach Mike Lonergan. "I love Warren. I've skied everywhere else, but I love Warren, and I love that flatbread place. Everybody saw what took place up here, and this happens to be a state I have had the opportunity of really enjoying, so I felt compelled to do something if we could because it seemed to go a little more under the radar than it should've nationally. I'm pleased to be a small part of it."

Cashman knows a thing or two about living through natural disasters.

"I grew up in Kentucky on a horse farm and experienced tornadoes," he said. "As a kid I experienced the worst tornado in the history of Kentucky. If you're in a position to help out, you do it. I wish we could've been up here sooner and the money could get to the people quicker. Times are tough, regardless of having a natural disaster thrown at you. It's a beautiful, wonderful state."

While many peppered Epstein with questions about his parting with the Red Sox ("I was looking for a new challenge, and the timing shifted a little bit. But I don't know how things would've changed had we made the postseason."), his Vermont ties shone through.

"Buster asked and it was a quick yes," he said. "I am a New Englander. It was horrible to see what the folks went through up here and anything we can do to help is well worth it. I have some ties to Vermont, my wife and I have friends who own a big farm in Pittsfield, and they went through a lot. There's a bit of a personal connection. But everyone down in Boston, when this was going on was following it and wishing there was something we could do to help, and now there is.

"Everyone's rallying around Buster and his efforts here. I've had a lot of people from baseball reach out and see what they can do to help. Hopefully it won't stop just with this event. A lot of times people think you raise a lot of money with an event and that's the end of it. Another disaster strikes and attention is placed elsewhere, but the reality is people here are going to need help for a long time. There's a lot of work to be done."

Other Vermont sports figures were also present, including senior Sports Illustrated writer and founder of the Vermont Frost Heaves Alexander Wolff, and Essex High School athletic director Ed Hockenbury Jr. and boys basketball coach Jeff Goodrich.

Pirates GM Huntington, who grew up in neighboring New Hampshire, spoke of how his older brother was unable to join the rest of the family at the event, ironically, because he was home milking his herd.

The talk shifted from Cashman's new three-year deal with the Yankees ("I'm still working that out with my therapist," he said.) to the September collapse by the Red Sox to the GM's biggest regrets in trades and the free agent market.

"We've always had a good relationship but now we can do business together," Epstein said. "We had very few direct trades for obvious reasons, but now I have the opportunity to do business with the Yankees and the Red Sox as well."

Fans questioned the guests about the pace of the game, whether Pete Rose will ever make it into the Hall of Fame, the impact life in baseball has on their families, the farm system, the new collective bargaining agreement, and their favorite memories from Little League.

As one of the youngest GMs in baseball, Epstein was asked for his advice for the younger set: "I think the most important thing when you're younger than most of your colleagues, is to treat them with respect with the understanding that in time you'll earn their respect and they'll return it back to you," he said.

With all the support Vermonters have given Major League Baseball, baseball returned the favor Saturday night in Randolph Center.

When somebody needs something, Vermonters don't wait around...

State regulators and legislators will face other dilemmas. In the weeks after Irene, environmental laws prohibiting the removal of gravel from rivers and streams were relaxed so that contractors could quickly obtain gravel to rebuild road beds and shore up banks. Those laws prohibiting the removal of gravel had been enacted for two reasons – some experts believed that gravel slows down river flow and removing it creates the risk of flooding; additionally, gravel in stream beds provides shelter and nourishment to fish and other river dwellers like mudpuppies that feed, hide and breed under these protected shallows. But in the wake of the storm, some environmentalist raised the question of whether the state had violated its own rules, not just causing environmental damage but creating the opportunity for future flooding by allowing so much gravel to be removed from streams and rivers. Of course, a lot of that gravel and debris had not been there before Irene, which realigned not just rivers but undermined dozens of river valleys, in some cases deepening and widening them, in other cases, depositing gravel islands in the middle of streams that could grow with the routine accumulation of silt and vegetation, creating new opportunities for log jams and flooding.

Additionally, engineering work to determine how to rebuild dozens of roads, a process that normally takes six to eight weeks and often involves community hearings and other time-consuming reviews, was done in-office in a matter of days. Here again, some environmentalists questioned the rapidity with which decisions were made and the processes used to get the work done. While few question the need to provide access to stranded communities, it seems likely that some of the hastily reconstructed roads will present problems as the seasons change. Snow and ice, plowing and sanding, spring melting and run-off, thawing and freezing – all of these will test the work of contractors, town employees and Agency of Transportation employees.

One thing that the Shumlin administration made clear, however, these shortcuts along with the cooperative efforts between towns, outside contractors and local residents helped to reduce the cost of rebuilding Vermont. While it was initially believed that the cost of getting Vermont's roadways open before winter would exceed $600 million, Shumlin's administration lowered the anticipated cost twice to roughly $100 million after federal assistance.

Beyond these concerns, more philosophical questions remain. As Gil Newbury, who headed up the Incident Command Center in Mendon, observed after three months of road reconstruction, the general philosophy in place was to rebuild roads where they had been to prevent even more disruption to communities than they had already received and where possible to put rivers back where they had been before Irene. Yet, there are places in Vermont and Route 107 is a prime example where even those rebuilding the roads wondered whether their work would be undone in another storm.

As Doug Casella, the contractor who has spent his life either demolishing or rebuilding roads and buildings after nature has had its way, said, "Anyone who thinks you can keep a river from going where it wants to go is dreaming."

Disaster struck
and
Vermonters rose up
in response.

Acknowledgements

In writing this book, I am humbled by the many people whose lives were turned upside down by Tropical Storm Irene but still managed to have time for me and other journalists at the Rutland Herald and Barre-Montpelier Times Argus who wanted to capture their stories. We share a deep appreciation and respect for what you have been through and the way in which you faced your disasters with courage and strength. Meeting and talking with you was an experience I will never forget.

I am indebted to Rob Mitchell, state editor of the Rutland Herald, who supported this project from the beginning and to Chris Morrow of Northshire Bookstore and Shires Press, who was exceedingly generous in helping us with this project. We could not have completed it without Deb Wraga, whose design work enhanced our words and photographs.

My debt to the writers and photographers at the Rutland Herald and Barre-Montpelier Times Argus is immeasurable. Not only did we include your stories and photographs in this book, and wish we could have included more, but your articles, photographs and videos that did not appear in this book informed me as I did my own reporting and writing. My job would have been impossible without your good work. It was also informed by the dozens of posted photos, videos and messages on YouTube, Facebook and other online resources.

Lastly, a thank you to Verandah Porche and Patty Carpenter, Susan Mordecai, Mary T. Holland, Mary McCallum, Jon Graham, Rep. Oliver Olsen, and Gov. Peter Shumlin for sharing your stories of Tropical Storm Irene.

Yvonne Daley

I echo Yvonne's words on the Vermonters I encountered while reporting on this story. You exemplified the best of my native state. Thank you to Yvonne for seeing this book through, and to the newsrooms of the Rutland Herald and the Times Argus - in the days and weeks following Irene you made me proud to be a journalist.

Rob Mitchell

PHOTOGRAPH PERMISSIONS

Yvonne Daley wishes to thank the following photographers featured in this book.
All images are copyrighted and can not be reproduced without the
photographer's and/or the Rutland Herald and Times Argus's permission.

Images *courtesy of Jeb Wallace-Brodeur — cover, A vintage Austin, 10, 40, 61-65, 76 cleanup in Waterbury & silt covers,
77 Waterbury underwater, 87 Sign up, 119, 144*

Images *courtesy of Vyto Starinskas — back cover, Sue Flewelling, pages 4, 13, 17, 22, 27, 28, 35, 42, 44, 54, 55-57, 77 Route 4,
87 outside home of Tracy Templeton, 109, 120*

Images *courtesy of Mark Collier — Gordon Gifford, a couple inspects, page 3*

Images *courtesy of Kevin O'Connor — pages 9, 11*

Images *courtesy of Cassandra Hotaling Hahn — pages 29, 32, 33, 49, 50, 52, 76 water covers Route 103*

Images *courtesy of Rick Russell — pages 47, 77 Quechee covered bridge*

Images *courtesy of AJ Marro — pages 77 Shaw's, 87 National Guard*

Images *courtesy of Yvonne Daley — Susan Mordecai photos, pages 87, Dot Pingree, 88, 101, 130*

Images *courtesy of Jessica Stratton 142, 143*

Jessica Stratton is rescued after spending four hours trapped in her car—

which had been swept against a tree by floodwaters in Grafton.

Family photos, Moretown, Vermont.